DEDICATED
BY THE

TANYA
in a nutshell

An easy-to-read synopsis to understand and review Tanya

Tanya In a Nutshell
ISBN: 978-1-945288-03-6
First Edition - Elul 5777 / September 2017
Copyright © 2017 by BSD Publishers

Author: Nadav Cohen
Cover Design & Layout: Carasmatic Design
Managing Editor: Mendy Weiss
Text prepared by: *Wellspring* PRESS

Published and Distributed by:
BSD Publishers
Brooklyn, NY
347-560-9770
Info@BSDpublishers.com
www.BSDpublishers.com

Printed in Ukraine

FOREWORD

W e have all studied the Tanya many times in the process of learning Chitas. One would imagine that after so many reviews, we would know it practically by heart. Yet, the fact is that most of us do not yet know the Tanya fluently.

One of the greatest challenges that stands in the way of remembering the Tanya is piecing the daily segments together. Tanya is like a very long maamar, in which each section leads into the next. When only studying a short segment each day, we struggle to retain the flow from yesterday's section, never mind reconstructing the build of the entire sefer.

To this end, we present you with a chapter-by-chapter synopsis of Tanya, so that you can grasp the basic outline of the sefer. Whether you are following the daily schedule of Chitas or another pattern, the synopsis offers a quick review and a general picture to assist in understanding the Tanya as a whole.

In addition, we have included several short inspirational thoughts on each chapter, to help the reader apply the study to daily life.

Since the study of Chassidus hastens the coming of Moshiach, it is our hope that the enhanced understanding of Tanya will usher in the coming of Moshiach, when the world will be filled with the knowledge of Hashem.

Nadav Cohen
Tzfas, Eretz Yisroel

GENERAL
BREAKDOWN

Chapters 1-8: *The Soul's Makeup*

Chapters 9-17: *Struggle of Two Souls*

Chapters 18-25: *Uncovering the Natural Love*

Chapters 26-34: *Finding Joy & Banishing Sadness*

Chapters 35-40: *Action vs. Meaning*

Chapters 41-50: *Levels of Love and Fear*

Chapters 51-53: *Resting of the Shechina*

OPENING PAGE

———～～～———

I n the opening page, the Alter Rebbe sets the general purpose of the Tanya: a book for mediocre people (*Beinonim*).

However, unlike it sounds, the *Beinoni* is not a modest level, but quite a great one. Most people aren't born to become *tzaddikim*, to completely banish their evil inclination. Those who override their natural inappropriate inclination, are called *Beinonim*.

"If Only a *Beinoni*"

The great *chossid* of the Mitteler Rebbe and the Tzemach Tzedek, R. Hillel of Paritch, after studying the Tanya said, "Until now I believed that I was a *Tzaddik*. Now, if only (*halevai*) I should be a *Beinoni*…"

This is also a common response of returnees to Judaism who are exposed for the first time to Jewish spirituality. As one man said:

"Before I discovered Torah and *mitzvos*, I sought out 'spirituality.' I would rise early each morning for 'spiritual service,' worked on helping others, and the like. When I started my journey to Judaism and started learning Tanya, I understood how lofty the demands of the Alter Rebbe are, and to what degrees of self-discipline a Jew is expected to reach. Until then I thought I was so great, now I realize how much I have to grow."

Very Close

The basis of Tanya is the *passuk* (Devarim 30:14), "For the matter is very close to you, in your mouth and in your heart, to do it." This short *passuk* carries so much depth. In Tanya, the Alter Rebbe explains how not only is the observance of *mitzvos* something 'close' and doable for every Jew, but even serving Hashem with one's **heart** by loving and fearing Him, is something that every Jew can achieve.

The Long Short Way

In the opening page the Alter Rebbe states that the purpose of this book is to explain how it is very close "in a long and short way." This is opposed to the "short and long way," which appears to be a shortcut, but turns out to be much longer because of stumbling blocks along the way. The path the Alter Rebbe is teaching appears to be longer since it is more thorough, but it then gets us to the destination smoothly, making it the quicker route.

INTRODUCTION

―――⧄⧄―――

"All the Answers to All the Questions!"

In his introduction the Alter Rebbe addresses a question which was on the minds of many: How can a book of advice replace hearing it from the Rebbe directly? And how can one book address all the varied issues and challenges in G-dly service?

The Alter Rebbe explains that the book is addressed to those he knows personally and is addressed to answer the questions that they asked him privately, and he included in this book "all the answers to all the questions."

Chassidim add, that the Alter Rebbe, with his *ruach hakodesh*, was able to foresee every person who studies Tanya throughout all the generations, and addressed their specific concerns in it.

One who cannot succeed in finding an answer to his issue in the Tanya, should ask the spiritual leaders of his community to guide him. The Alter Rebbe warns those leaders not to feign humility, claiming not to understand the Tanya either. Instead they should guide all those seeking guidance, and by doing so Hashem will enlighten them and reward them.

Time does not allow to reply to each and every individual in person.

The Alter Rebbe writes that since he did not have the time to speak with each person individually, he was therefore writing the Tanya.

CHAPTERS 1-8:
THE SOUL'S MAKEUP

Chapter 1: *Every Jew has two souls, the first of which is from kelipa.*

Chapters 2-5: The G-dly Soul

Chapter 2: *The second soul is literally a part of G-dliness.*

Chapter 3: *The ten faculties of the soul, the emotions are a product of the mind.*

Chapter 4: *The garments of the soul (thought, speech and action), the primary way to connect to Hashem is through these garments.*

Chapter 5: *The advantage of Torah study over all other mitzvos.*

Chapters 6-8: The Animalistic Soul

Chapter 6: *The Animalistic Soul, its faculties and garments.*

Chapter 7: *Permissible items can be elevated when used for the sake of Heaven.*

Chapter 8: *Forbidden items cannot be elevated even if used for the sake of Heaven.*

CHAPTER 1
Two Souls

————⚬⚬⚬————

In the first chapter, the Alter Rebbe raises several questions from Mishna and Gemara on the common understanding of a *Beinoni* ("the mediocre one") as one who has half merits and half transgressions, and explains instead that it refers to a person who commits no sins at all.

In the course of the Tanya, the Alter Rebbe will explain that the difference between a *Beinoni* and a *Tzaddik* can only be understood after an appreciation of the various levels of G-dly service. In the twelve chapters that lead up to the answer, the Alter Rebbe explores the Chassidic perspective of the Jew's essence: What are the forces that function within a Jew? What does Hashem expect of a Jew? How should a Jew utilize his faculties to achieve Hashem's Will?

At the end of the first chapter, the Alter Rebbe lays down the foundation of all G-dly service: every Jew has two souls. Not just two inclinations, but two separate souls.

The first soul is rooted in *kelipa*, the impure and mundane spiritual forces, and is comprised of four elements (fire, wind, water and earth) from which all bad traits originate. Yet, it is a form of *kelipa* called "*noga*" (lit. light) which contains good as well, and is expressed in the instinctive Jewish traits of mercy and kindness. Whereas the souls of other nations come from a lower *kelipa*, and therefore their kindness is tainted with personal interest.

> ### Rabba said, "I, for example, am a *Beinoni*." Abbaye replied, "If so, my master does then not leave life for any other creature."
>
> *The sage Rabba, who was on a lofty spiritual level, defined himself as a Beinoni. His student Abbaye was thus telling him, "You are not allowing anyone else to live, since if you Rabba, who are on such a great level, are only a Beinoni, then everyone else who are lower than you is a Rasha, a sinner."*

CHAPTER 2
The G-dly Soul

———～～～———

In the second chapter the Alter Rebbe defines the essence of the G-dly soul, the *neshama*: it is literally a part of G-dliness, of the Creator Himself.

He employs three metaphors for this: (1) The *neshama* comes from Hashem's blowing a 'deep breath.' Unlike the rest of creation which comes from G-dly 'speech,' the *neshama* comes from deep within Hashem. (2) The *neshama* comes from Hashem's 'thought,' which is higher than speech. (3) The *neshama* is like a son who is a part of his father.

To elaborate: The source of all *neshamos* is from the 'Supernal *Chochma*' (*Chochma* of the spiritual world of *Atzilus*), and only by passing through the various levels in its descent to this world, do differences develop between various *neshamos*. This is similar to a fetus which originates from the father's brain, and is formed into distinct limbs during the nine months in the mother's womb. Now, just as the limbs of the child

17

are connected to his brain, which is turn is connected
to the brain of his father, all Jewish souls are connected
to the *tzaddikim* of the generation (our brain) who are
connected to Hashem's *Chochma* (our father's brain).

This is the meaning of the teaching, "Whoever
cleaves to sages is considered to have cleaved to the
Shechina itself," since cleaving to the sages actually
connects the Jew with his source, the *Shechina*.

Since the level of the soul is set according to its
process of descent, it is possible for a great soul to be
born to ordinary parents. However, the 'garment' of
the G-dly soul, through which the G-dly soul connects
with the animal soul and the body and thereby fulfills
mitzvos, depends on the parents' spiritual state at the
time of conception. The holier they act, the greater the
'garments' will be.

> **"This matter [that Hashem and
> His wisdom are one] is impossible
> for a human to fully understand,
> as it is written, 'Can you discover
> the depth of Hashem?'"**
>
> *You can't understand how Hashem, His wisdom,
> and everything He created are one? That's fine. It
> can't be understood. As finite human beings, we
> are unable to grasp matters such as these which are
> beyond our understanding.*

CHAPTER 3
Faculties of the G-dly Soul

The G-dly soul is comprised of ten faculties, which correspond to the ten supernal "*sefiros*" with which Hashem created the world.

These faculties can be divided into two categories: intellect and emotions. The intellect is made up of three intellectual faculties: *Chochma* – Concept, *Bina* – Analysis, *Daas* – Connection. The emotions are seven: *Chessed* – Kindness, *Gevura* – Severity, *Tiferes* – Beauty, *Netzach* – Endurance, *Hod* – Splendor, *Yesod* – Foundation, *Malchus* – Royalty.

Chochma – Concept is the kernel of an idea, *Bina* – Analysis is the development of the idea into a logical theory, and *Daas* – Connection is connecting to the concept and internalizing it.

Chochma and *Bina* are called the 'parents' of the emotions. When a person contemplates the greatness of

Hashem, he gives birth to emotions of awe and love for Hashem to the point of expiration.

Daas sustains the emotions, since without total focus and attachment to the concept, it is impossible to generate genuine emotion, and whatever feeling is fleeting and fantasy.

Contemplation

In the third chapter we learn about one of the fundamental foundations of Chabad thought: the mind creates the emotions. Therefore, it is important to learn about and understand the greatness of Hashem. The more we understand, the more we will feel. To this end, it is necessary to study in-depth (Bina), and not suffice with knowing the core concept (Chochma). The more we analyze the details, the deeper impact it will have on our emotions.

However, study alone is not enough, and it is necessary to connect to the concept (Daas). We have to ask ourselves: "How does this concept relate to me?" "What difference does it make to my life?" Without a personal connection, the study won't affect real change, and the influence will be fleeting.

CHAPTER 4
Garments of the G-dly Soul

*A*side from the ten faculties, the G-dly soul also has three 'garments.' These 'garments' differ from the faculties in the fact that they are not part of the soul, but like a garment which the soul 'puts on' and 'takes off.' These garments are **Thought**, **Speech** and **Action**, and they function to express the intellect and emotion of the soul.

The concept of this chapter is that although the garments are not a part of the soul, it is specifically through these garments that we can achieve a connection to Hashem. Performing a physical *mitzvah* is infinitely greater than feeling love or fear of Hashem.

This idea is based on a general understanding of Torah and *mitzvos*. The Alter Rebbe teaches that Torah and *mitzvos* are not just a set of laws to guide us in how to act, but rather it is the wisdom and will of Hashem which is one with Hashem Himself. Hashem invested Himself into the Torah, and then gave Himself to us as a gift. Through studying Torah and performing *mitzvos* we can connect to Hashem.

Since the primary objective of learning Torah and fulfilling *mitzvos* is to achieve a true connection to Hashem, there is in this sense no difference between a scholar who understands a page of Gemara with great depth and a simpleton who performs an uninspired *mitzvah*. Both connect to Hashem with an incredible connection.

The physical performance of a *mitzvah* in this world is loftier than the spiritual reward for the *mitzvah* which the soul receives in *Gan Eden*. In *Gan Eden*, there shines just a ray of the *Shechina*, whereas when we perform a *mitzvah* in this world, we grasp Hashem Himself.

> ### Wherever you find the greatness of Hashem, there you will find His humility.
>
> *The simple meaning of this statement is that when describing Hashem's greatness, His humility is also mentioned. The Alter Rebbe explains it deeper: What is Hashem's greatness? His humility. Meaning, His ability to limit His infinite self into the Torah in order that we could connect to Him. That is greatness!*

CHAPTER 5
Torah Study

When we fulfill a *mitzvah* we draw down a G-dly light upon ourselves, as if Hashem 'hugs' us, but we do not become one and internalize with the G-dly light. However, when we study Torah, our minds become one with the G-dly light that is enclothed in the Torah, since when we understand the Torah, our intellect is 'wrapped' in Torah and the Torah is 'wrapped' in his intellect. When we also mouth the words of Torah and physically move our lips, we draw upon ourselves an additional G-dly light.

In this chapter, we learn that studying Torah for its own sake, *lishma*, means in order to connect thereby to Hashem. Studying in order to be honored or to sharpen the mind is surely not *lishma*. Even studying to know how to perform the *mitzvos* is still not for its own sake. True study *lishma* means to study for no other purpose than to cleave to Hashem as He is found in the Torah.

As it is written, "And Your Torah is in my innards."

The simple meaning in this verse of Tehillim is that even our eating (that which enters our innards) is in accordance with Torah.

Here the Alter Rebbe adds a deeper dimension that the Torah itself is the 'food.' Just as the body is nourished with food, the soul is nourished with Torah. Through studying Torah and "digesting" it, the Torah becomes one with him, as food becomes a part of the body and becomes one entity with it.

CHAPTER 6
The Animalistic Soul

———— ∾∾∾ ————

*A*fter explaining in chapters 2-5 the character of the G-dly soul, the Alter Rebbe moves on to explain the animalistic soul. He first notes that the faculties of the animalistic soul are parallel to the G-dly soul: ten faculties, comprised of intellect and emotion, and three 'garments' – thought speech and action. However, the essence of the animalistic soul is ego, being independent from Hashem.

The Alter Rebbe explains a fundamental principle in Chabad philosophy: Holiness can only reside with one who is *battel*, selflessly united with Hashem to the extent that he doesn't view himself as a separate existence. Of course, even those who aren't *battel* to Hashem receive their energy from Him, since everything must receive life from Him. However, he receives his life from Hashem's external energy (*achorayim*). In other words, this energy has passed through so many contractions and changes, that the receiver doesn't feel that the energy is from Hashem.

This is why the sages say that evil prevails in this world. Since the G-dly energy is so limited and hidden, the unholy forces are able to rule.

The unholy forces (*klipas*) are divided into two categories: (1) *shalosh klipas hatmeios* ('three impure *klipas*)' – which contain no holiness at all, and they give life to non-Jews, non-kosher animals and foods, and to all forbidden thoughts, words and actions. (2) *klipas noga* ("*kelipa* of light") – which will be explained in the following chapter.

> **However, whatever is not subservient to Him... does not receive its life from Hashem's holiness... only from the "back."**
>
> *Whoever isn't subservient to Hashem receives his energy in a "backhanded manner," like one who is compelled to give something and throws it over his shoulder. (For example, when having to pay a ticket, one will often push off paying it until the last day, and then give it with anger and insult.)*

They are all actions that are performed under the sun which are all vanity and bad spirit.

Not only are sins called "vanity and bad spirit" (Koheles 1:14), but even all permissible actions which are done for personal interest, and not for the sake of Heaven are also called "vanity and bad spirit".

CHAPTER 7
Klipas Noga

⌘

The second level of the unholy forces is *klipas noga* ("*kelipa* of light") which contains an element of good. This *kelipa* gives life to the animalistic soul of a Jew, and all permissible objects. This force serves as an intermediate between holiness and impurity.

When a permissible object is used according to regulations of the Torah and for a G-dly purpose, it is elevated to holiness. When it is used for an un-G-ly purpose, then the object together with the user are drawn into *klipas hatmeios*. The user must then do *teshuva* and return to serve Hashem, which then allows the sparks of energy which descended to *klipas hatmeios* to return to holiness.

If an action was done that is contrary to Torah's regulations, *teshuva* cannot elevate those sparks, and they will remain in *kelipa* until the coming of Moshiach. An exception to this is *teshuva* done out of intense love for Hashem which causes sins to be transformed into merits.

The sins are transformed into merits since they are what brought him to such an intense love.

One day during Tishrei, a young man showed up at a Chabad House, and told the rabbi that he had come to join them for Yom Kippur. Although he considered himself secular, he was particular to observe Yom Kippur, and to spend the day in shul in fast and prayer. However, the rabbi was distressed to notify him that he had miscalculated, and Yom Kippur had already passed...

The young man was shocked at having missed Yom Kippur. He was more moved by his missing the fast, than he had in all his years of observing it. His pain moved him to come closer to Hashem, and eventually he made a complete return to Torah and mitzvos.

CHAPTER 8
Impure Klipas

———⁓⁓———

In this chapter, the Alter Rebbe explains the negative effect of eating forbidden foods which come from the '*shalosh klipas hatmeios.*' In this scenario, intent plays no role; even if he unintentionally used the forbidden object with holy intentions, it cannot be elevated to holiness (only if a person later repents with extraordinary '*teshuva* of love' he can elevate those forbidden forces).

In order for a soul to be freed from the forbidden forces, it must undergo a cleansing in accordance with the type of wrongdoing it did. Even use of the permissible *klipas noga* without appropriate intention requires cleansing.

Studying secular knowledge (not for the sake of Heaven) impurifies the soul more so than empty chatter or other pleasures, since secular knowledge impurifies the mind, while other pleasures impurify only the emotions. Only one who studies secular knowledge so he can have livelihood and through that properly serve

Hashem or for other G-dly purposes can elevate them to holiness.

The energy in it cannot go up and enclothe itself in the words of Torah and prayer.

Forbidden foods are tied up in the control of kelipa (the Hebrew word for forbidden, ossur, also means tied). That is why good intentions cannot elevate the sparks contained in them. From this we can learn the importance of strictly kosher food. Even if they were eaten unknowingly, they will not be elevated.

CHAPTERS 9-17:

THE STRUGGLE OF TWO SOULS

Chapter 9: *The G-dly soul wants full control of the body and its faculties.*

Chapter 10: *The definition of a "Tzaddik Vetov Lo" and a "Tzaddik Vera Lo."*

Chapter 11: *The definition of a "Rasha Vetov Lo" and a "Rasha Vera Lo."*

Chapter 12: *The definition of a Beinoni.*

Chapter 13: *The nature of a Beinoni, three levels.*

Chapter 14: *Every person can become a Beinoni, one should aspire to become a Tzaddik.*

Chapter 15: *Service of Hashem means toiling beyond one's standard capabilities.*

Chapter 16: *Love of Hashem that isn't felt in the heart.*

Chapter 17: *Explaining the passuk, ki karov eilecha hadavar me'od, "For this thing is very close to you, in your mouth and in your heart, that you may do it."*

CHAPTER 9
Struggle of the Souls

After describing each of the souls, the Alter Rebbe proceeds to explain the struggle that takes place between them. But first he explains the "map" of the souls, where in the body does each soul reside.

The place of the G-dly Soul is primarily in the mind, and from there it influences the 'right side' of the heart and the rest of the body. The Animalistic Soul resides primarily in the 'left side' of the heart, and from there it influences the mind and the rest of the body.

What is the aspiration of each of the souls? To have full control of the "miniature city" – the human body. Most of this chapter describes the desire of the G-dly Soul who wishes that the body be permeated only by G-dly intellect, emotions and 'garments' (thought, speech and action). Meaning the mind and heart of the body should be used to contemplate the greatness of Hashem, to generate intense feelings of love and fear which can transform the Animalistic Soul to love

Hashem as well. Then, all the person's thoughts, words and actions will be of holy nature.

At the end of the chapter, the Alter Rebbe mentions briefly that the Animalistic Soul desires the exact opposite. In truth, even this contradictory desire is for the person's good, since by overcoming the challenges set by the Animalistic Soul he will reach even greater heights.

"She desires the exact opposite."

This describes the essence of the Animalistic Soul and allows us to identify it: whatever is holy, the Animalistic Soul desires the exact opposite...

CHAPTER 10
Tzaddikim

━━━━━━━ ∼∾∼ ━━━━━━━

Here the Alter Rebbe begins to offer answers that he presented in the first chapter.

In this chapter the Alter Rebbe explains the inner meaning of a *Tzaddik* and its various levels, a "*Tzaddik Vetov Lo*," a *Tzaddik* who knows only good, and a "*Tzaddik Vera Lo*," a *Tzaddik* who knows evil.

A *Tzaddik* is one who has overcome the struggle between the souls. The G-dly Soul has overpowered the Animalistic Soul, and the heart serves the G-dly Soul only. That is a result of the fact the *Tzaddik* has such intense love for Hashem, and a corresponding disgust for anything not done for Hashem. Not only does he not desire anything forbidden, he doesn't desire anything which isn't G-dly.

A "*Tzaddik Vera Lo*" still has some evil within him, but it is inconsequential and irrelevant in comparison to his good. This is a result of the fact that his love for Hashem is incomplete, and his disgust for anything un-G-dly is likewise not absolute. Another difference between them is the fact that "*Tzaddik Vera Lo*" serves Hashem to satisfy his thirst for G-dliness, unlike the "*Tzaddik Vetov Lo*" who does it for the sake of Hashem alone, without any personal interest, however lofty.

Love for Hashem leads to disgust of evil.

To use a parable: A minister who loves the king and admires him will naturally hate the king's enemies. The greater his love for the king, the more he will hate the enemies. So too, the more a person loves Hashem, his hate for the klipas which conceal Hashem rises.

CHAPTER 11
Resha'im

━━━◦⌇◦━━━

In chapter 11 the Alter Rebbe explains the inner meaning of a "*Rasha Vetov Lo*," a *Rasha* who knows good, and a "*Rasha Vera Lo*," a *Rasha* who knows only evil.

By a *Rasha*, his Animalistic Soul has overpowered the G-dly soul and rules the heart and mind, and as a result, he sins in thought, speech and action. An advanced "*Rasha Vetov Lo*" has good in his heart, yet it is subservient to the evil within him (contrary to a *Tzaddik* whose evil is subservient to his good). His sins are irregular, and are generally only 'light' sins. When he does sin, he regrets it and does *teshuva*. A lower "*Rasha Vetov Lo*" transgresses more severe sins and does so more often, however, he still regrets his sins and returns.

A "*Rasha Vera Lo*" no longer has any good in his heart (the opposite of a "*Tzaddik Vetov Lo*" who has no evil). Therefore, when he sins he does not regret it.

Nevertheless, he is a Jew and still has a G-dly Soul, but it "surrounds him" *(makif)* and is not sensed by him.

"Thoughts of sin are worse than sin itself."

The 'garment' of thought is more refined than the 'garments' of speech and action, and therefore, a blemish of thought is more severe. Just as you can't compare dirtying an ordinary garment to dirtying a fine silk garment.

CHAPTER 12
The Beinoni

Now the Alter Rebbe explains the inner state of a *Beinoni*, who is between a *Tzaddik* and a *Rasha*. He is not a *Tzaddik* since he hasn't eliminated his natural inclination for bad. He is also not a *Rasha* since he has raised himself to a state where it is inconceivable for him to sin in action, speech or even thought.

When he *davens*, he contemplates Hashem and banishes all evil desires from his heart. However, after *davening* the evil returns and he desires evil again. Yet, since by nature the mind can control the heart, he is able to control his feelings and not allow them to express themselves in thought, speech and action.

The effect of *davening* on the *Beinoni* helps him control himself from even thinking evil thoughts. An evil thought may enter his mind, but he immediately pushes it out of his mind. Similarly, when it comes to interpersonal *mitzvos*, he can control himself and not let his mind think thoughts of hate or anger towards someone who wronged him.

"He has never sinned and will never sin in the future."

The question can be asked: If a Beinoni is one who has never sinned before, how can someone who has sinned become a Beinoni? Moreover, how is Tanya, also titled by the Alter Rebbe as the "Book of Beinonim" if only one who has never sinned can become a Beinoni?

The words "he has never sinned" is not an account of his past, but a description of the Beinoni's current state of mind: he is incapable of seeing himself sinning in his past or in the future. Just as an ordinary observant Jew cannot fathom eating on Yom Kippur and doesn't need to struggle with his yetzer hara to restrain himself, so too, the Beinoni cannot think of committing any sin, big or small. Thus, psychologically "he has never sinned and will never sin."

CHAPTER 13
Three Types of Beinoni

There are two souls active within the *Beinoni*. When a person invests effort to strengthen his G-dly soul over his Animalistic one, he merit a Divine light which has the power to banish evil instantaneously just as 'light' chases away intense darkness without struggle.

The *Beinoni* must always remember that he has a force of evil within him, and not mistakenly think that he is a *Tzaddik* who rid himself of all his evil. Even during *davening*, when he feels a love for Hashem, his evil force is only "asleep," to be reawakened soon after, unlike a *Tzaddik* who is completely free of evil.

One type of *Beinoni* is a businessman, who evil thoughts do enter his mind, but through his effort and the assistance from Above, he right away chases all such thoughts from his mind. Another *Beinoni* studies Torah all day, and generally evil thoughts don't even enter his mind, but he doesn't generally feel love for Hashem. A third *Beinoni* is in a spiritual state of "*davening*" all day, not allowing the Animalistic Soul to express itself, and he feels love for Hashem most of the time (although he still does have evil in his heart, just that it is always 'asleep').

Although the love that the *Beinoni* feels during *davening* passes afterwards, it is nonetheless real, relative to his level of G-dly service.

ANSWERS

to questions listed in chapter 1

Should a person see himself as a *Rasha*, which may lead him to melancholy, or not, which may lead to frivolity?

A person should view himself "like a *Rasha*," meaning as a *Beinoni* who has evil leanings in his heart which he must overcome, and not like a *Tzaddik* who has no evil at all.

(In chapters 31 and 34 the Alter Rebbe explains how to ensure that this self-image should not lead to sadness, though the Tzemach Tzedek notes that the answer is not obvious due to the lengthy explanation).

How did Rabba think that he was a *Beinoni* if in truth he was a *Tzaddik*?

In his humility, Rabba thought that he still had evil within him. He figured that the evil didn't act up since he studied Torah all day and it was therefore "asleep."

CHAPTER 14
Every Person Can Be a Beinoni

———— ～～ ————

E very person is naturally capable of regulating his thought, speech and action, and can thus be a *Beinoni*. Even though he still has evil leanings in his heart, he can overpower them and not allow them to take action.

This is accomplished through contemplating how even an unscrupulous Jew (*kal shebekalim*) will generally sacrifice his life to sanctify Hashem's name. Though he may not observe *mitzvos*, when faced with a choice to die or abandon his faith, he will choose to die.

Why then does he perform sins which separate him from Hashem? Because a *ruach shtus* (spirit of foolishness) hides the fact that sinning separates him from Hashem. By realizing this true effect of sin, we can overcome all challenges and serve Hashem daily, refusing to transgress and become separate.

To truly detest evil is only possible for a *Tzaddik*, yet we are expected to work in that direction. How can we do this?

1) By designating times to consider the emptiness of worldly pleasures, and how they ultimately become waste and worms. This will bring us to temporarily disgust worldly pleasures.

2) By training ourselves to rejoice with Hashem by contemplating Hashem's greatness according to our ability.

Though these emotions of disgust for worldly pleasures and joy for Hashem are not totally genuine, we should nevertheless pursue them, since:

1) We must do all we can to fulfill our oath to "become a *Tzaddik*."

2) Over time, habit becomes second nature.

3) Perhaps Hashem will grant us a spirit from a *Tzaddik* and we will truly reach these levels.

"Even when the heart desires ... he can overcome ... telling himself, 'I don't want to be a *Rasha*.'"

Until now the Alter Rebbe followed a path of contemplation. In this approach, a person considers Hashem's greatness, which brings him to love and fear Hashem, which then motivates him to follow Hashem's commandments. Why here, when explaining how every person can become a Beinoni, does he advise a different approach (an approach explained at length later in chapters 18-25): to consider how sins separate him from Hashem, something which he strongly does not want? Why isn't it enough to use the mind to rule the heart through contemplation?

The answer is that although in these chapters the Alter Rebbe is explaining how it is possible to serve Hashem with love and fear by the use of contemplation, nevertheless when someone has an urge to sin, he doesn't have the ability to contemplate at length and arouse fear of Hashem to stop him from sinning. Since in this chapter the Alter Rebbe is giving us the formula how to be a Beinoni "at all times," he mentions how to refrain when tempted to sin, by quickly considering how a sin separates him from Hashem.

CHAPTER 15
G-dly Service

———— ✺ ————

In G-dly service there are two levels: "One who serves Hashem" – a *Beinoni* who struggles and overpowers his Animalistic Soul, and "one who doesn't serve him" – a *Beinoni* who has almost no struggle, since his Animalistic Soul is naturally inclined to study and isn't interested in worldly pleasures. He is therefore lacking in G-dly service.

To explain: Exertion that is beyond a person's in-born capabilities is worth far more than his normal activities. In the days of the Gemara they would study a chapter 100 times, and one who studied it 101 times, just one more than the norm, is called a "one who serves Hashem."

Likewise, the *Beinoni* who doesn't exert himself against his Animalistic Soul does not **serve** Hashem. Only when he rises above his nature, does he earn the title of "one who **serves** Hashem" and then his service is deemed "complete." If he does not go against his nature, and just does whatever is demanded of him (which is possible through his "Hidden Love" described in chapters 18-19), he is performing an incomplete service.

Oved Elokim

A Beinoni who struggles and overpowers his Animalistic Soul is called "One who serves Hashem," in Hebrew "Oved Elokim." Chassidus explains that aside from the simple meaning as one who serves Hashem, it can also be translated to mean: one who works on and 'fixes' Elokim.

The meaning of this: Elokim refers to a level of G-dliness that is limited. Through struggling and going out of one's limitations, he draws down Hashem's infinite light into the level of 'Elokim.'

CHAPTER 16
The Beinoni's Principles

───··∾∾··───

Until now we explained how the *Beinoni* controls his thought speech and action ('garments'), but not his internal emotions like a *Tzaddik*. It would seem that a *Beinoni* is incapable of effecting his emotions and can only change his 'garments.' In this chapter the Alter Rebbe explains that in order for a *Beinoni* to maintain full control over his 'garments' he must arouse emotions of love and fear for Hashem by contemplating Hashem's greatness.

Another rule: There are some *Beinonim* who do not succeed in arousing an emotional love for Hashem, only a "hidden love." Such a person can still be a *Beinoni* through contemplating Hashem's greatness and coming to a strong intellectual conviction how he ought to love Hashem, and conducting himself accordingly. In place of an **emotion** motivating the action, he has an

understanding and firm **resolution** that it is appropriate to cleave to Hashem entirely through Torah and *mitzvos*.

When doing so, a person has the advantage of true emotions which are invested in action. Hashem attaches the resolution to the action, and considers it as if he had the appropriate emotions.

"This is what Hashem desired."

Even if contemplation doesn't bring you to have emotional longing for Hashem, the very fact that you understand how you should feel and you conduct yourself in line, this is considered a "complete service."

This is very encouraging, especially for our generation, when we see how difficult it is to elicit feelings as a result of contemplation. We should not despair over the fact that we don't have an emotional connection. We need only understand how we should feel and translate it into action, and it's as if the emotion is there.

CHAPTER 17
"Ki Karov Eilecha"

———∽∽∽———

*A*t this point we can summarize the "Long Way" and explain how it is very near for every Jew.

One would think that "*bilvavcha*," changing the feelings of the heart is not near for every Jew. However, by rearranging the words, the *passuk* teaches us how this is possible.

In line with the normal process, the word "*bilvavcha*," in your heart (emotions), should have been listed first, followed by "*b'ficha*," in your mouth (speech), and "*la'asoso*," to do it (action). Instead, the *passuk* inserts "*bilvavcha*" right before "*la'asoso*" to imply that the only feeling required here is one which brings to action. Every person can understand Hashem's greatness to the extent that he will follow His instructions in practice.

"*Resha'im* are controlled by their hearts."

When our sages say that "Resha'im are controlled by their hearts" they are referring to completely evil people who have no noticeable element of goodness (Rasha Vera Lo). As punishment for his conduct, he loses control over his heart.

How can such a person ever become a Beinoni?

Indeed, for such a person it isn't enough to regret his actions and resolve to do good in the future, rather he must be pained by his lowly spiritual state and "break" his coarseness. This will enable him to regain control over his heart and eventually become a Beinoni.

CHAPTERS 18-25:
UNCOVERING THE NATURAL LOVE

Chapter 18: *Every Jew has a natural love to Hashem which is expressed in faith and mesiras nefesh.*

Chapter 19: *"The candle of Hashem is the soul of man."*

Chapter 20: *The deeper meaning of G-dly Unity.*

Chapter 21: *There is no separate entity from Hashem, even the concealment of Hashem is Him.*

Chapter 22: *The concealment of Hashem is only from our perspective, a strong concealment creates the klipas.*

Chapter 23: *Torah and mitzvos are the inner will of Hashem, and they unite a Jew with Him.*

Chapter 24: *Sins separate us from Hashem just like Avoda Zara (idolatry).*

Chapter 25: *Summary: fulfilling mitzvos is very near when we arouse the natural love within us.*

CHAPTER 18
Very Near

⌇⌇⌇

This chapter begins a new section of Tanya which explains how it is "very near" to become a *Beinoni* even for someone who is incapable of practicing contemplation.

This can be done by arousing the "hidden love" which exists in the heart of a Jew. It is an "inheritance" from our forefathers, the *Avos*, and is found by every Jew regardless of his level or observance.

The source of this love is *Chochma* of the *neshama*. *Chochma* is the source of intellect, and is the point of contact between G-dliness and the soul, and it therefore contains the pure faith which supersedes logic.

It is this faith that causes a Jew to sacrifice his life to sanctify Hashem's Name, since he would rather forego all material life so as not to be separated from Him. Revealing this nature doesn't require deep and extensive contemplation about Hashem's greatness.

"Because I approach You like an animal – I am always with You."

Trying to comprehend that which is higher than logic will prove unsuccessful. Only by living with faith and rising above logic (thus being in a sense "like an animal"), can we be "with You," with Hashem alone as He is above logical comprehension.

CHAPTER 19
Chochma of the Soul

―――――❦―――――

To further explain the "hidden love" inside a Jew, the Alter Rebbe draws a parable from a fire which is naturally drawn upward. All creatures want to assert and reinforce themselves. The only exception is fire which longs to eliminate its identity and be nullified in its source above.

Likewise, the *neshama* longs to ascend and become one with the Creator, even if doing so will cause it to lose its identity. This has no logical explanation; it's simply the nature of a *neshama*.

This nature comes from the soul's faculty of *Chochma* which expresses nullification, *bittul*. It is the sign of whether something belongs to *kedusha* or to *kelipa*: In *kedusha* everything senses *bittul* and doesn't feel separate from Hashem. Something that feels separate is *kelipa*.

This spark of *Chochma* is present in every Jew, even if he isn't observant. However, the manifestation of

Chochma which animates the rest of the soul with *bittul* is in "exile." The essence of *Chochma*, which cannot be exiled, is "asleep."

As long as we are occupied with material matters, we don't feel our spark of *Chochma*. But when we encounter a test in faith where we are pressed to abandon *Yiddishkeit*, the essence of that spark becomes revealed and it permeates all the other faculties. That is why even a non-observant Jew can withstand a test of faith, since he doesn't want to be separate from Hashem.

The spark of *Chochma* is very powerful. When revealed, it pushes away *kelipa* from affecting even just the soul's external 'garments' of thought, speech and action.

Mesiras Nefesh of a Jew

Even if contemplation doesn't bring you to have emotional longing for Hashem, the very fact that you understand how you should feel and you conduct yourself in line, is considered a "complete service."

This is very encouraging, especially for our generation, when we see how difficult it is to elicit feelings as a result of contemplation. We should not despair over the fact that we don't have an emotional connection. We need only understand how we should feel and translate it into action, and it's as if the emotion is there.

$\mathcal{A}$NSWERS

to questions listed in chapter 18

What is the source of the "hidden love?"

Chochma of the soul.

How did we receive it as an 'inheritance' from our forefathers?

Our forefathers, the *Avos*, were subservient to Hashem like a "chariot" (*merkava*) and thus their descendants inherited a G-dly soul that naturally loves Hashem.

What is the character of this love?

It causes the *neshama* to nullify itself to Hashem and to forego its own identity.

How is fear included in this love?

Because of the 'natural love' the *neshama* has, it not only wants to connect to Hashem, but also fears becoming disconnected from Him.

CHAPTER 20
G-dly Unity

———— ∞ ————

To enable us to reveal the spark of *Chochma* in day-to-day life, the Alter Rebbe explains how the first two commandments of the *Aseres Hadibros* ("*Anochi*" – I am Hashem, "*Lo Yihyeh Lecha*" – Do not serve idols) include all of the *mitzvos*. "*Anochi*" includes all the positive commandments, and "*Lo Yihyeh Lecha*" includes all the negative commandments.

To understand this, we must first understand the concept of Hashem's unity. Beyond the basic belief that there is only one G-d Who created the world, we also believe that there is no other entity at all besides Him.

The creation of the world did not cause any change in the oneness of the Creator, and He is the only entity now exactly as He was before He created the world, since the G-dly "words" that created the world are insignificant to Him, thus making the world itself totally insignificant to Him. The insignificance of the world to Hashem is analogous to a single utterance of a person's speech: a single utterance means nothing to the person himself. Similarly, the world which was created by the "word of Hashem" does not have any significance to Him in any way.

There are several levels to this:

1) The insignificance of the **one utterance** to the **infinite faculty of speech**, which is infinitely greater in quantity.

2) The insignificance of **spoken words** to words of **thought**, which are of a much higher quality.

3) The insignificance of **spoken words** to the essence of the soul where there are no words at all.

Hashem is Everywhere

As a young boy, the Rebbe Maharash enjoyed carving wood with a penknife. Once, a chossid approached him with an offer, "If you tell me where Hashem is, I will give you my expensive penknife." The boy retorted, "If you can tell me where Hashem isn't, I will give you my knife!" The chossid was pleased with the reply, and gave him the knife.

CHAPTER 21
Ein Od Milvado -
Nothing Aside from Him

In the above-mentioned parable of speech there are two features:

1) It reveals that which was hidden in a person's thought. So too, Hashem's "speech" expressed itself in creating the world.

2) Speech becomes separate from the person who spoke the words. This feature is not applicable to Hashem's speech, since nothing leaves Hashem, and everything is continuously connected to Him. It follows that all creations are not separate from Hashem, and are therefore not independent entities from Him.

Despite the fact that nothing is 'separate' from Hashem, we don't feel it. Hashem wanted that we should feel ourselves to be separate and independent entities, in order that we should be able to exist. If we would feel our source, we would be completely nullified in it, and we would be unable to carry out our mission to fulfill *mitzvos* and reveal Hashem in the physical world. To this end, Hashem limited and concealed His light from us.

This concealment only affects us but not Hashem, since the concealments themselves come from Him, they don't pose a true disguise for Him. As the *passuk* says, "Hashem is *Elokim*," that even the concealments that result from the level of "*Elokim*" comes from Hashem Himself.

"Even darkness can't hide from You."

Darkness cannot hide Hashem since it too is from Him. An example for this is found in the halacha that a man may not use his own hand as a head covering, since part of the person is not considered a "covering."

The Ceiling Beam

On the final day of his life, the Alter Rebbe laid in bed with his grandson at his side. The Alter Rebbe turned to his grandson and said, "You see that beam in the ceiling? I'm telling you that I don't see a 'beam.' I see only the G-dly energy, the word of Hashem, which is giving it life."

CHAPTER 22
Multiple Concealments

In the previous chapter, the power for creation was compared to speech in two ways: (1) it reveals that which is hidden (in thought), and (2) it becomes separate from its source. It was explained that the second aspect cannot be applied to Hashem, since it is not possible for anything to become separate from Hashem.

In this chapter, the Alter Rebbe explains that this separation is nevertheless relevant for us, since we indeed feel separate. In order to create that perceived separation, Hashem concealed Himself on multiple levels.

As a result of these concealments, *klipas* which contradict the oneness of Hashem, came into being. Yet, they too receive their life force from Hashem. The difference between *kelipa* and *kedusha* is that *kedusha* is Hashem's Inner Will, the purpose for which the world was created. *Kelipa* is from the external will, meaning that they were only created to enable the true purpose of creation to actualize. Hashem gives life to *kelipa* in an unwilling manner, from His "back," like someone who must give something to his enemy and hands it to him from behind his back while looking away.

Furthermore, this external energy does not become internalized in the *kelipa*, but influences it from a "distance." As a result, they don't feel how their life force comes from Hashem, and they believe that they are independent of Him. While a small amount of G-dly energy does permeate the *klipas*, it is in "*galus*" within them, and they therefore don't recognize that it comes from Hashem.

This is why our sages say that "arrogance is comparable to idolatry." When a person is arrogant, he shows that he considers himself a separate 'entity' from Hashem. Thus, although he may believe that Hashem is the ruler of all existence, he fails to believe that Hashem is the only true existence and nothing is independent of Him.

"Just to punish the *resh'aim* and give reward to the *tzaddikim*."

Hashem is not interested in the kelipa as an end for itself, and He created it only to provide man with free choice between good and evil. This is the significance of punishment for resh'aim and reward for tzaddikim.

"For holiness does not reside only upon that which is subservient to Him."

In chapter 6 the Alter Rebbe stated this without explanation. Here he explains it: a created being naturally feels itself to be independent. This perception is false since he receives his entire life force from Hashem. However, since this is its perception, it is not a vessel for holiness.

CHAPTER 23
Torah and Hashem are One

―――――∽∽∾――――

*A*fter explaining that the contractions and concealments on Hashem's Inner Will are the cause for *galus* and feeling of independence from Hashem, the Alter Rebbe now explains how this Inner Will is found in Torah and *mitzvos* and how it unites a person with his creator.

Mitzvos are described in Zohar as "limbs of the King," since just as limbs are receptacles of the soul energy, *mitzvos* are receptacles of Hashem's Will.

This unity through fulfilling *mitzvos* has three levels:

1) The limb that fulfills the *mitzvah* is subservient to Hashem like a chariot (*merkava*) is subservient to the rider. A chariot has no will of its own at all, and is totally submissive to its rider. Still, it is only subservient to the rider, and not one with him.

2) The power of action which performs the *mitzvah* (the energy in the hand) unites with the Will of

Hashem, like limbs are united with the soul energy in it. Though the limbs and the soul are separate entities, they nevertheless unite to the extent that the limbs immediately respond to the soul's wishes.

3) The person's mind that understands Torah, his speech, and his neshama, become totally united with Hashem. They are not two separate entities that are tied together, but they become one entity.

In this respect there is an advantage to Torah study in this world over the G-dly light that shines in the spiritual worlds. The G-dly light in Heaven is only a ray of Hashem's will and intellect, while we connect with those levels themselves through the Torah. Specifically, it is because of this world's downside that we can't feel the Torah's spiritual light. We have the advantage of being able to study the Torah in its purest form, whereas above, where they feel the light, they cannot handle the intensity of the Torah itself.

Through the study of Torah we draw upon ourselves a loftier fear (*yirah ila'ah*), which cannot be accessed through the fulfilment of *mitzvos*.

CHAPTER 24
Ultimate Separation

———— ◦◦◦ ————

*A*fter explaining at length the unity of man and Hashem through Torah and *mitzvos*, the Alter Rebbe now explains the other side of the coin: the separation of man from Hashem through sin, G-d forbid.

Mitzvos, it was explained, are the Inner Will of Hashem and therefore unites a Jew with Him. Conversely, sins are the opposite of Hashem's Will and the ultimate concealment over it, and they therefore cause the sinner to become separate from Him. While sinning, the thought, speech or action which are performing the sin, as well as the person's Animalistic Soul which is enclothed in those faculties, become attached to *kelipa*.

Essentially, one who sins is worse than *kelipa* itself, since *kelipa* doesn't transgress Hashem's Will, and is only doing what it was commanded. However, one who sins is acting against Hashem.

That is why our sages said that "one doesn't sin unless a spirit of foolishness enters him." If a person recognized that sin separates him from Hashem, he surely wouldn't transgress. When put to a test of renouncing his faith, a Jew can control himself, since he refuses to be separated from Hashem. Thus, if not for the "spirit of foolishness" which deludes him into thinking that he won't be separated, he would never sin.

There is a difference between those sins for which there is *kares* (punishment of disconnection from Hashem) and other sins both with regards to the G-dly Soul and the Animalistic Soul:

1) The Animalistic Soul becomes disconnected from Hashem at any sin, and it descends to the *klipas hatmeios*. Yet, after an ordinary sin it immediately returns to holiness, whereas after a *kares* sin it remains disconnected until the person does *teshuva*.

2) The G-dly Soul is completely disconnected only through a *kares* sin, and it remains disconnected until the person does *teshuva*. With an ordinary sin, the G-dly Soul's connection is only slightly blemished, and during the actual sin it is in severe "exile."

Temporarily placing the G-dly Soul in exile is also a terrible thing, just as taking the king by his head and placing in a filthy toilet, is an incredible disgrace, even if just for a short moment.

"A mosquito preceded you."

In the hierarchy of creations, the mosquito stands very low, being capable only of 'receiving' and not of 'giving' (it ingests food but does not excrete it). When a person sins, he is lower than a mosquito which never transgresses the Will of Hashem.

CHAPTER 25
Sanctifying Hashem's Name

Now, we can better understand the quote on the opening page of the Tanya, "Because the matter is very close to you, in your mouth and in your heart, to do it."

In chapter 17 the question was asked: How can developing the emotions be "very close" when it seems to be possible only for outstanding individuals?

Based on the previous chapters we can understand it. Every Jew has a concealed love for Hashem, which is revealed at times when he is challenged to renounce his faith. Since every sin is like idolatry and every *mitzvah* is an expression of faith, we can arouse our natural love for Hashem to observe every *mitzvah*. We can remove the foolish spirit which conceals this reality, by just remembering that we are Jews and would be ready to sacrifice our lives for Hashem.

In this manner, we can overcome forbidden desires, since we would be willing to suffer tortures which are far more painful than passing a desire. Likewise, we can commit ourselves to fulfilling positive *mitzvos* with enthusiasm and labor, and overcome the laziness of the Animalistic Soul.

The Alter Rebbe also answers another question we may have: Why should we work so hard to abstain from sin if even after sinning we can return?

The answer is that the same argument could be made with idolatry, and yet we are ready to sacrifice our life not to be separate even for a moment! Therefore, by equating all sins to idolatry, we won't want to sin even for a moment.

This will help us understand why Moshe Rabbeinu commanded the Jews before entering *Eretz Yisroel* about reciting *Shema* twice a day. *Shema* discusses accepting the yoke of Heaven to the point of self-sacrifice. Why was it necessary to arouse self-sacrifice when they were promised that no one would stand in their way when they conquered the land?

Rather, the self-sacrifice that was demanded of them wasn't for fighting national enemies, but for the eternal battle with the inner enemy—the Animalistic Soul. Arousing readiness for self-sacrifice would help them overcome their day-to-day struggles in serving Hashem in the new land.

A Most Important Chapter

This perek gives us the most important tool to overcoming the yetzer hara. Because of its importance, the Rebbe's father told the Rebbe to learn it on the day of his wedding, stressing that he should not learn it in depth, but rather with much kavana.

CHAPTERS 26-34:

PRACTICAL ADVICE IN SERVING HASHEM

Chapter 26: *Advice for sadness from material difficulties or from sins.*

Chapter 27: *Advice for sadness from bad thoughts which arise throughout the day.*

Chapter 28: *Advice for sadness from bad thoughts which arise while davening or learning.*

Chapter 29: *Advice for a closed, unmoved heart.*

Chapter 30: *Making a reckoning in comparison to others.*

Chapter 31: *Advice for sadness which results from the reckoning.*

Chapter 32: *Ahavas Yisroel which results from the G-dly soul's joy.*

Chapter 33: *Joy from contemplating Hashem's unity.*

Chapter 34: *Joy from being a home for Hashem through fulfilling Torah and mitzvos.*

CHAPTER 26
Joy in Serving Hashem

*A*fter explaining how it is "very close" to serve Hashem with our heart, the Alter Rebbe enumerates some issues that can stand in the way of serving Hashem, and are important to avoid.

The first subject is joy and sadness.

In order to overcome our Animalistic Soul, we must be energetic—which results from joy—and not lazy—which results from sadness and worry. When two people wrestle, the energetic one will usually win, even if he isn't stronger.

Although there are sources that indicate that sadness has an advantage, it's not the sadness that's good, but the true joy that follows it. Through occasional sadness with certain guidelines, a person can break the barrier that separates him from Hashem that was created by his sins. Then, he will be truly joyous from being close to Hashem.

We can rid ourselves of being sad from material difficulties by changing our perspective. In the spiritual realm, everything is good. Moreover, those things that to us seem "bad" actually have an even loftier source in the spiritual worlds than things that are openly good. Therefore, bad things are actually a reason for **rejoicing**, since through them a person becomes connected to a higher level of G-dliness.

Sadness from past sins during *davening* or learning is not good. Although it seems to be an arousal to *teshuva*, it is simply a trick of the *yetzer hara* to stop us from serving Hashem with joy.

Even if sadness from sin comes to us during mundane activities, it is still a ploy of the *yetzer hara* to pull us down and draw us into pleasures. Otherwise, why would we suddenly start thinking of our spiritual state in middle of work?

Therefore, when these thoughts come to us in middle of the day, we should push them out of our mind. Instead, we should designate special times to consider our spiritual wrongdoings. At that prearranged time, we should do proper *teshuva* and believe with a full heart that Hashem forgave us. Being reunited with Hashem through *teshuva* will cause us great joy.

"Just as he blesses on the good."

The Mishna states, "Just as one recites a blessing on the good, he should recite a blessing on the bad." The Gemara explains that this doesn't mean that one should use the same wording for both, since each one was assigned its own unique bracha, but rather that one should recite the bracha with the same emotion, and accept his troubles the same level of joy.

CHAPTER 27
Bad Thoughts

*A*nother cause for sadness can be bad thoughts that enter our mind. Even if we push them away, the mere fact that we have such thoughts can sadden us, since according to our understanding we shouldn't be having such thoughts at all.

The Alter Rebbe explains that only true *Tzaddikim* don't have any bad thoughts. The rest of us will always have bad thoughts, and our job is to fend them off. Instead of causing us to feel sad, we should be happy to fulfill a *mitzvah* of not dwelling on forbidden thoughts. This is the task of the *Beinoni*: to constantly avoid bad thoughts, words, and actions.

This process of struggling with bad is called "*iskafya*" (subduing), and it causes Hashem tremendous pleasure. Another form of pleasure to Hashem comes from the service of *Tzaddikim* who transform bad into good, "*Is'hapcha*."

These two forms of service are comparable to two very different types of foods: the pleasant service of *Tzaddikim* is like sweet tasting foods, and the challenging efforts of *Beinonim* are like sharp and spicy foods, which can be even tastier.

Even by elevating ourselves just a little (such as delaying a meal to subdue our Animalistic Soul), a great holiness descends upon us from Above.

"That is why Iyov said 'You created *Resha'im*.'"

In this chapter, the Alter Rebbe concludes the answer to the question he raised in Chapter 1: How could Iyov say that Hashem forms who will be a Rasha when man has free choice regarding his conduct?

The answer is that Hashem doesn't create anyone to be a Rasha. Rather, He determines who will only be a Beinoni (and not a Tzaddik) and will undergo the same challenges as a Rasha – to struggle with evil thoughts and desires.

"His sadness comes from arrogance that he doesn't recognize his place."

The sadness discussed in this chapter results from a person thinking that he is close to the level of a Tzaddik, and he should therefore not have such thoughts. By recognizing his true level, that he is far from the level of a Tzaddik, he will rejoice at the opportunity to perform a mitzvah.

CHAPTER 28
Disturbance During Davening

A bad thought which plagues us during mundane activities can more easily be seen as an opportunity to fulfill the *mitzvah* of pushing it away. But if a bad thought come to us while *davening* or learning, one can seemingly still have good reason to be sad, since ultimately these thoughts are disturbing his service of Hashem, by not even letting him *daven* properly.

The answer offered here is that we must know that these thoughts indicate that our *davening* is going well, and we must ignore the bad thoughts completely. *Davening*, according to its inner meaning, is a time when we uncover our G-dly Soul and arouse feelings of love and awe towards Hashem.

When we do this service properly, the Animalistic Soul is afraid to lose his influence over us and he responds with an attack. Therefore, specifically the bad thoughts during *davening* indicate that our *davening* is successful, which is why the Animalistic Soul feels the need to respond. This should only inspire us to strengthen our *davening*.

If a person would have been comprised of one soul which is sometimes inclined towards good and sometimes to bad, then having bad thoughts would indicate that the person is now negatively inclined and his *davening* is not good. However, the truth is that a person has two separate souls – an Animalistic Soul and a G-dly Soul – and the fact that the Animalistic Soul is drawn to bad doesn't show negatively on the G-dly Soul.

If we do not succeed in ignoring the bad thoughts, we should plead with Hashem to help us, just as a father has mercy on his children. Moreover, Hashem is helping Himself, as it were, in overcoming evil.

"For example a person who *davens* with concentration and an evil man talks to him to disturb him."

A person should recognize that the only reason that an evil thought occurs to him during davening is in order to distract him. He should ignore it, just as he would ignore a person who approaches him during Shmoneh Esrei with the express intention of disturbing him.

"To have mercy on him as a father has mercy on his children."

A person should ask Hashem to help him get rid of his evil thoughts. Yet, he should not come in his own merit, as that may put him up for judgment whether he is indeed worthy. Instead, he should simply ask for mercy as a child of Hashem. This will arouse Hashem to help the person on His own account.

CHAPTER 29
A Dulled Heart

~~~~~

In this chapter, the Alter Rebbe addresses another common problem that plagues many people seeking to serve Hashem properly: *timtum halev* – a dulled heart, in which the heart is closed to spiritual inspiration – preventing the person from *davening* properly.

The reason that our heart doesn't respond to what our mind understands is because of the heart's natural arrogance. By making a sincere reckoning and realizing where we truly stand, we will feel lowly in our eyes and break our heart's arrogance, and our heart will then "open."

Even a true *Beinoni* can realize that, despite his accomplishments, his consciousness is dominated by the Animalistic Soul. This places a person far from Hashem, since the Animalistic Soul is drawn to forbidden things, and is thus lower than those forbidden things themselves (see Ch. 24). Even if during *davening* he has some degree of sincere love for Hashem, the fact that it disappears after *davening* indicates that it is not thoroughly genuine.

If this contemplation doesn't move this *Beinoni*, he should consider the sins of his youth and the blemish he caused to the spiritual worlds. Although much time has passed since he committed those sins, nonetheless since the spiritual worlds are beyond time, it is as if he had made those blemishes today. Even if he has done *teshuva*, the fact that presently his heart is stopped-up indicates that his past *teshuva* is incomplete, and his past sins still separate him from Hashem.

Even someone who has never sinned in his life should make a reckoning of his thoughts, words and actions which were unrelated to Hashem, during which time he served as a vehicle for *kelipa* (see Ch. 6). Likewise, he should realize how most of his dreams concerned foolish matters, and that had he sanctified himself properly during the day, his dreams would have been holy. After considering all of this, a person will be disgusted by his Animalistic Soul, he will degrade it and not allow it to assert itself above the G-dly Soul.

Another solution is to attack the Animalistic Soul in his thoughts with a loud and raging "voice." Like darkness, *kelipa* is not a true existence but rather an absence of light. By condemning the Animalistic Soul, the truth that it is nothing will be revealed, and it will dissolve in the presence of the G-dly Soul.

When the spies spoke badly about *Eretz Yisroel,* Moshe did not argue with them; he only stated firmly how Hashem was upset at them. With that, he destroyed the brazenness of their Animalistic Souls which had taken hold of them, and allowed their essence—"believers sons of believers"—to be revealed.

CHAPTER 30
True Humility

━━━━◆◆◆━━━━

It is possible that even after contemplating how low and far we are from Hashem, we may still feel proud when we compare ourselves to those around us. In this chapter, the Alter Rebbe enables us to fulfill the instruction to "be humble before every person," even those who are seemingly lower than us in G-dly service.

To honestly fulfill this instruction of our sages, we must preface another one of their instructions, "Do not judge your fellow until you reach his place." It is that person's place or circumstance that causes him to sin. He may be in a bad environment, or he may have a negative nature and is easily impassioned toward forbidden pleasures. Of course, he himself cannot justify his own conduct, but others must conclude they are even lower since they can't contain themselves from transgressing a much easier test. Additionally, the more Torah a person studies and the greater his G-dly service, the more is expected of him.

Considering all of this will enable us to truly feel more humble than any other person. That humility will break our arrogance and unclog our heart.

> ## "And to be of lowly spirit before every other person with genuine sincerity."
>
> *When a person realizes that others possess qualities that he doesn't have, he will become humble, but he won't have the 'lowly spirit' that is needed to break the arrogance of the heart. Only when a person truly feels that his fellow is actually greater than him, and that he doesn't even overcome easier tests than those that his friend has to deal with, will he have a "lowly spirit."*

CHAPTER 31
Sadness vs. Bitterness

———— ∿ ————

It would seem that thinking about our lowly state would make us sad, which is contrary to the joyfulness we are trying to attain. In this chapter, the Alter Rebbe explains why this should not concern us.

Firstly, sadness, when used suitably at designated times, has a certain advantage in that it cracks the shell that covers our heart and allows us to become aroused to the service of Hashem. We fight the *kelipa* with its own forces, using sadness, a negative trait, to break our ego.

Secondly, the sadness from being distant from Hashem is not really sadness (*atzvus*) but bitterness (*merirus*). Sadness highlights the fact that we are far from Hashem and leads us to become depressed and give up hope. Bitterness highlights how our G-d given mission is incomplete, and elicits strong willpower to change and move forward.

An opportune time for bitterness is when we already feel dejected about our material challenges. We can transfer that sadness to spiritual bitterness, thereby letting go of our physical distress (since in comparison it won't seem so important), and become motivated to change.

Then, we should consider the following: "Despite my sorry spiritual state which is a result of my Animalistic Soul, I have a G-dly Soul which is being imprisoned." This thought will arouse within us such pity for our G-dly Soul and motivate us to set it free and return it to its true standing.

This return, as well as all of a person's G-dly service, should be accompanied by a sense of joy at reuniting our G-dly Soul with Hashem, like a prince who was taken captive and was at last freed and reunited with his father, the king.

Although a *Beinoni's* body and Animalistic Soul were not transformed to good, this is not a reason for sadness. Since the G-dly Soul ought to be so much more important to us then our Animalistic Soul, we should not allow the sadness over the state of our Animalistic Soul get in the way of joy at the freedom of our G-dly Soul.

"The suitable time [for sadness] is when he is already sad from physical matters."

We find that drinking wine can cause G-dly joy. Although the natural elatedness that follows drinking wine is from the Animalistic Soul, nonetheless that paves the road for arousing the G-dly Soul to joy. Likewise, when the Animalistic Soul is in a mode of sadness it can be utilized for spiritual reckoning and growth.

CHAPTER 32
Ahavas Yisroel

———∿∿———

*A*fter explaining how the G-dly soul ought to be much more important to a person then his Animalistic Soul, the Alter Rebbe continues to explain how this attitude is also the optimal route towards fulfilling the *mitzvah* of truly loving a fellow Jew to the same degree as one loves himself.

The difficulty with truly loving another person results from the body and Animalistic Soul, which causes us to feel distinct. However, from the perspective of the G-dly Soul, not only may the other person's soul be even greater than our own, moving us to love their soul even more then own - moreover, all G-dly Souls are really one as all Jews are like brothers, in their original source in Hashem, they are not separate entities at all.

Consequently, when our body is primary and our soul is secondary, we cannot truly love another person. But if we make our soul primary and our body secondary, we can see beyond the bodies, and unite with the other. That is why *Ahavas Yisroel* is called, "the essence of the Torah," since all of Torah is about highlighting the G-dly Soul.

Furthermore, through Torah we draw down Hashem's Infinite Light into the Source of the Jewish Souls, and that is only possible when the souls are united.

This does not contradict how Torah instructs us to despise a Jew who sins. First of all, that is referring to a Jew who is of the same spiritual standing as ourselves, and we have tried speaking lovingly to him out of his bad ways, and yet he does not try to improve. In all other situations, we must increase our love towards that person. Even if it doesn't bring the desired results, nothing will be lost, since we have in any case fulfilled a *mitzvah* to love a fellow Jew.

"Those who consider their body primary and their souls secondary."

If our own body is important, then when we look at another person we will focus on their body. But if our own soul is most important to us, then when we will automatically focus on other people's souls, which will enable us to truly love them.

CHAPTER 33
Ultimate Joy

nother way to refine our souls is by contemplating Hashem's Oneness – how He is in every place at all times just as He was before He created the world, and therefore was not affected by the creation of the world, since He is everywhere and therefore His "words" that created the world are totally nullified within Him. When one believes in the above, he becomes "close" to Hashem. He thus fulfills the entire purpose of the creation – namely, to make oneself a "vessel" in which Hashem can reside by believing in the true oneness of Hashem.

Realizing how through this belief Hashem is so close to us can cause us much joy. If a great king came to stay with a simple and ordinary citizen, that man would feel elated. How much more so, should a person rejoice when he realizes that Hashem resides and dwells within him, as it were. Moreover, this closeness came to us as an inheritance, without any effort on our part, because the belief in the true oneness of Hashem is something natural to every Jew.

This joy enables us to overcome all the challenges we face in fulfilling Torah and *mitzvos*. The prophet Chavakuk stated that all that we need to fulfill the Torah is to have excitement about our faith. When we have a strong sense of joy resulting from our faith in Hashem's presence with us, we are motivated to fulfill all the *mitzvos*.

An even greater joy results from the knowledge that by us believing in Hashem's oneness we overpower the *kelipa* and cause Hashem pleasure. This is especially so outside of *Eretz Yisroel* where the darkness is even stronger. The light that comes from within darkness is superior and causes Hashem greater joy, as it were.

> **"He should also rejoice doubly over his faith, especially outside of *Eretz Yisroel* which is impure."**
>
> *Even when the faith inside the heart of a Jew is "asleep," it has the power to overcome evil. The Baal Shem Tov explains that Jews were dispersed in far-flung places across the world to elevate those unholy places, and when a Jew passes through those places, the "sleeping" faith in his heart purifies that environment.*

CHAPTER 34
A Home for Hashem

———— ❧ ————

In the previous chapter, the Alter Rebbe explained how we can rejoice from being close to Hashem as a result of contemplating Hashem's true Oneness. In this chapter, the Alter Rebbe explains how we can increase the closeness and joy through connecting all our faculties with Hashem.

Total unity of all the faculties with Hashem's Oneness is reserved for great *Tzaddikim* such as the *Avos* and Moshe Rabbeinu who were selflessly subservient to Hashem and a vehicle (*merkava*) for His will. When ordinary Jews experience a G-dly revelation, such as at the Giving of the Torah, their souls escaped their bodies, since they could not bear the great light. Hashem therefore commanded the Jews to build a *Mishkan* where He would dwell amongst them in a manner they could withstand. Ever since the *Beis Hamikdash* was destroyed, Hashem rests within us through the study of Torah.

When we consider our current situation, we will recognize that we are far from the level of the *Avos*, and the only way for us to become a vehicle for Hashem is by studying His Torah. The fact that we can become a dwelling place for Hashem is a source of great joy.

To be a dwelling for Hashem, one should be particular to set aside time in the morning and night to learn Torah. To remain connected to Hashem throughout the rest of the day, there are three solutions:

1) To have the strong will and desire to study Torah all day. Hashem then considers it as if we had actually studied all day.

2) By giving a portion (particularly a fifth) of our earnings to *tzedaka*, we elevate all our work and earnings to be a dwelling place for Hashem. This is similar to the effect of a *korbon* in the *Beis Hamikdash*: bringing an animal sacrifice would elevate all animals in the world, and a flour offering would elevate all vegetation.

3) By using the energy from food and other material needs for serving Hashem, we elevate those things to holiness and make them a dwelling place for Hashem.

In the previous chapters we have laid out five reasons for the G-dly Soul's joy when serving Hashem: (1) Being liberated from imprisonment by the body through doing *mitzvos*. (2) Fulfilling the purpose of its descent into the body by refining it (Ch. 31). (3) Being close to Hashem's Omnipresence. (4) The ability to cause

Hashem pleasure by our actions (Ch. 33). (5) Becoming a dwelling place for Hashem (Ch. 34).

All these forms of joy do not negate feeling humble. The joy is because of the loftiness of our G-dly Soul, whereas the feeling of lowliness is because of our Animalistic Soul (Ch. 31).

A Percentage of the Whole

When one gives to tzedaka a percentage of his earnings, since it is based on the total amount that he earned, it is considered as if all of the money assisted him in giving that specific amount. This is why when giving a portion of our earnings to tzedaka, we elevate all our work and earnings to be a dwelling place for Hashem.

SUMMARY
Sadness and Joy

CHAPTERS 29-31, 33-34

───※───

Chapter 29

Timtum Halev, a stopped-up heart, is when the heart is closed to spiritual inspiration because of pride. We must break the pride of the Animalistic Soul by making a thorough and honest reckoning, or by attacking it forcefully.

Chapter 30

Further reckoning leads us to the conclusion that we are inferior even to those people who are seemingly far lower than us.

Chapter 31

Reckoning can lead us to sadness and bitterness which "breaks" the Animalistic Soul. We must emphasize the joy in fulfilling mitzvos which allows the G-dly Soul to leave spiritual imprisonment. Another reason for joy is the G-dly Soul fulfilling its purpose in its descent to this world to elevate the Animalistic Soul.

Chapter 33

The path to ultimate joy is by contemplating that Hashem is close to us because of our belief in Hashem's Oneness and He rejoices over our actions.

Chapter 34

Since the destruction of the Beis Hamikdash, Hashem rests primarily upon one who studies Torah. One who studies Torah should rejoice over being a dwelling place for Hashem.

CHAPTERS 35-40:

*A*CTION VS. *M*EANING

CHAPTER 35
Comfort for the Beinoni

———— ✿ ————

In the previous chapters the Alter Rebbe advised on how to overcome sadness, blockage of the heart and to attain joy. Now, he will begin to explain in depth the final word of the *passuk* "*ki karov*" – "*la'asoso* – to do it." That expression implies that the most important thing is action.

This is a comfort for the *Beinoni* who can only correct the 'garments' of his Animalistic Soul – thought speech and action, but not the Animalistic Soul itself – his intellect and emotion.

Hashem rests only where there is complete attachment and nullification to Him. Since the true reality is that nothing exists aside from Him, the only way to connect to Him is by not living as a separate existence.

Emotion is an expression of our self and it can therefore not grasp Hashem. Even the lofty love for Hashem of a total *Tzaddik* is an expression of his personal appreciation and want. In the words of *Chassidus*, "*yesh mi she'ohev*," there is someone—a separate entity—who loves.

True nullification is only possible through fulfilling the Torah and *mitzvos* given to us by Hashem. These are one with Hashem and do not conceal Him, and when a person fulfills them this is not an expression of his personal want, rather he is setting himself aside to fulfill Hashem's will.

This advantage is even greater with fulfillment of practical *mitzvos* ("*la'asoso*"). When studying Torah, *Elokus* settles primarily upon the G-dly Soul and its refined faculties of thought and speech. Whereas when we perform physical acts with our body, we engage the Animalistic Soul as well, so that they all connect to Hashem.

A parable for this is the light of a candle. To produce a smooth flame, oil is fed into the wick, which becomes burnt up in the fire. Likewise, for the light of the *Shechina* to shine upon a physical body, he must provide oil to sustain its flame. Since a *neshama* is ultimately its own entity it cannot serve as the oil, and only *mitzvos* which are totally nullified to Hashem can be burnt up in His flame.

This is an encouragement for the *Beinoni*. Although he can't refine his inner self as a *Tzaddik* can, he can nevertheless connect to Hashem through fulfilling practical *mitzvos*, and thereby connect his body and Animalistic Soul as well. Though his mind and heart are not transformed, they nonetheless have a (forced) part in the *mitzvah* and the *Shechina* rests upon them too.

In the following chapters, the Alter Rebbe explains how the ultimate purpose of creation is the refinement of the world in which the *Beinoni* has a part.

A Non-Practical *Mitzvah*

Love and fear are also mitzvos, and one who loves and fears Hashem isn't just expressing his natural emotion, but he fulfills Hashem's will, and there is also no 'concealment' of Hashem. Nevertheless, love and fear of Hashem lack the advantage of practical mitzvos, for no physical act is being performed (similar to the study of Torah).

CHAPTER 36
The Purpose of Creation

After explaining in the previous chapter how practical *mitzvos* are greater than learning Torah because of their effect on the Animalistic Soul and the physical body, the Alter Rebbe continues to how refining the Animalistic Soul and body is actually the ultimate purpose of creation.

The purpose of creation is as the Midrash states, "Hashem desired a dwelling place in the lower realm (*dira betachtonim*)." Hashem's will was to "dwell" and reveal Himself specifically in the lowest and physical world.

Before creation, all that existed was Hashem alone. In truth, now too He is the only existence, and the change is only from our point of view. In the higher spiritual worlds, where there is less concealment, Hashem is felt more, and in lower spiritual worlds where the concealment is greater, He is felt less. In our physical world, the concealment is greatest and Hashem is not felt at all, to the extent that it is possible to deny His existence completely.

This process of concealment is part of Hashem's perfect plan. His intent with creating our lowly world was that He should be revealed here too. His pleasure comes from the transformation of darkness to light – when we discover Him in the most hidden places.

With the approaching redemption, Hashem will be revealed in His full glory. Although, such a revelation would normally cause the world to become naught, the Torah fortifies us so that we can contain it as we continue to exist.

At the giving of the Torah the souls of the Jews "flew out of them" since they were not yet fit for such a revelation, but through the Torah that they were given then, they had the strength to contain this great revelation and continue to exist. While the *Cheit HaEgel* (sin of the Golden Calf) brought back the concealment, the Torah and *mitzvos* of Jews throughout the ages made the world fit to contain the G-dly revelation at the ultimate redemption.

> **"The ultimate purpose is in the lowest world, since that was His will to derive pleasure from the breaking of the *kelipa* and the transformation of darkness to light."**

Hashem's desire was that specifically in this material world where klipas – who conceal and fight Hashem – are in power, a Jew should illuminate the darkness by serving Him. This transformation is the purpose of all the lofty spiritual worlds.

Now we can understand why the world was made so lowly and dominated by evil and klipas, since it is specifically the transformation of evil that Hashem desires.

Exile and Redemption

Galus is a situation where Hashem is hidden; geula is when He is completely revealed. That revelation is the purpose for which the world was created. At its core, even the world itself isn't intended to conceal Hashem, but rather that Hashem should be revealed throughout the world.

CHAPTER 37
Refining the World

———∽∾∽———

In this chapter the Alter Rebbe continues his explanation on the purpose of creation, and explains how that purpose is achieved through our actions. The revelation of Hashem when Moshiach comes is not a reward for our good deeds, but a direct result of what we do. Each *mitzvah* reveals Hashem in this world, though it won't be obviously seen to all until Moshiach comes.

How do our *mitzvos* refine the material world so that they don't conceal Hashem's presence?

When we do a *mitzvah* with physical items—*tefillin* with animal hides, *lulav* and *esrog* with vegetation—their materialism is no longer a cause of concealment, but a source of revelation. As mentioned in the previous chapter, *mitzvos* are the greatest source of G-dly revelation, thus, when an object is used to fulfill a *mitzvah*, it becomes a vessel for G-dliness.

Likewise, the energy of the Animalistic Soul with which the *mitzvah* was performed is also refined and elevated to holiness. Even the study of Torah entails a measure of physical activity since one is required to mouth the words which is also an action. Moreover, the food and drink which provided the energy are elevated as well.

The Animalistic Soul of a Jew and permissible material objects receive their life-force from *klipas noga*, whereas forbidden objects receive their life-force from the *shalosh klipas hatmeios* (see Ch. 6 for elucidation). When a Jew utilizes material objects to serve Hashem, he incorporates the *klipas noga* to holiness. Since *klipas noga* is the lifeline of the *shalosh klipas hatmeios*, once it is transformed into holiness the lower *klipas* will expire and cease to exist.

Every Jew has a portion in this world which he must refine, and collectively, Jews refine the entire world. When the world is completely refined, there won't be any more *klipas*, and nothing will conceal Hashem's presence.

This is the reason for the *neshama's* descent to this world. The *neshama* itself was fine beforehand, and it only descended below to carry out its mission of refining the Animalistic Soul and the world, and thereby bring the ultimate *geula*.

Our sages say that *tzedaka* brings the redemption. Unlike other *mitzvos* which refine just one part of the body and the Animalistic Soul, *tzedaka* impacts the entire soul. This is because of two possible reasons: (1) The person's entire self worked hard to earn the money that was donated to *tzedaka* (other *mitzvos* use only a specific function to carry out a specific task). (2) The money could have been used to buy things that are vital for his very existence (such a food).

Although Torah study does not refine the physical world the way *mitzvos* do, nonetheless Torah study has the advantage of elevating the inner elements of the Animalistic Soul, since it involves the person's thought and speech – which are more essential than action – and the mind itself.

Another advantage to Torah study is that the G-dly energy it draws down is greater. Just as the mind contains a higher form of life than the limbs, so too, Torah which is likened to Hashem's "mind" expresses a higher revelation than the *mitzvos* which are likened to Hashem's "limbs."

Yet, despite its advantages, action is primary, because the physical world is elevated primarily through physical *mitzvos*. That is why if a *mitzvah* opportunity which only we can do arises while we are studying Torah, we must interrupt our study to carry out the *mitzvah*.

Because Torah study accesses the loftiest levels of G-dliness, it is referred to as "calling" (*kriah*), since we call the highest levels of Hashem to come close to us through Torah study.

By recognizing that Torah study brings us Hashem Himself, we can attain a superior level of awe for Hashem, *yirah ila'ah* (see end of Ch. 23).

"The reward for a *mitzvah* is a *mitzvah*."

The simple meaning in this statement is that if we perform one mitzvah we will then merit to perform another. A deeper meaning is that the spiritual reward which we receive for a mitzvah is not something different which is given to us as reward, rather it is the G-dly energy of that very mitzvah.

Since the essence of a mitzvah is Hashem's Will, and the act of the mitzvah involves a physical object, thus when we do a mitzvah we inject the G-dly Will into the object which we are using.

This is what will happen in the geula – Hashem's Infinite Light will be revealed in this physical world.

CHAPTER 38
The Significance of Feeling

━━━━◦◦◦◦━━━━

*A*fter explaining the significance of practical *mitzvos* which create a dwelling place for Hashem and bring about the Final Redemption, the Alter Rebbe now explains how feeling and intent while performing a *mitzvah* are also necessary.

The difference between the G-dly energy generated by practical action and that of intent, is similar to the difference between the energy of the body and that of the soul. The body itself also has a G-dly spark so that it should exist (like all inanimate objects), however, the life of the soul which enters the body is far greater.

Though the G-dly energy of both the body and the soul are concealed, there is still a difference what level of G-dly energy resided in them. The energy that enlivens the soul is more and far greater than the energy that sustains the body.

More specifically, the G-dly energy can be divided into four levels which correspond to the four letters of Hashem's name *Havaya*, and this translates into four types of creations: inanimate matter, vegetation, animals, and humans.

A similar hierarchy exists in the way we perform a *mitzvah*:

1) Practical action – inanimate matter.

2) Speech and thought (e.g. Torah study) – vegetation.

3) Instinctive emotion – animal.

4) Intellect-borne emotion – human.

The higher form of G-dly service is when we feel emotion towards Hashem as a result of conscious thought and reflection. Like humanity which has intelligence and can practice free choice, this person chose his emotions based on his intellectual understanding.

The lower level is when a person fans his inborn emotions – *ahava mesuteres*, the hidden love with the fear that it includes (see Ch. 18-19). Like an animal which acts instinctively without the regulation of intellect, this Jew expresses his natural inherited emotions without exercising intellectual contemplation.

Dira Betachtonim:
Action and Emotion

Hashem doesn't only want physical mitzvos alone, he also wants the feeling for the mitzvah. A home has two features: (1) it is a space where the essence of the person resides (unlike other places where the person is there only for a side reason, and therefor only his external elements are found there), (2) a person can live and express himself unrestrained in the most revealed way. The act of the mitzvah draws down Hashem Himself, but the brightness and revelation comes primarily from doing the mitzvah with emotion.

CHAPTER 39
The Reward for Feeling

———— ❧ ————

In this chapter the Alter Rebbe continues his discussion on the various levels of feeling in *mitzvos*, and explains the impact of each type of feeling on the *neshama* that preforms the *mitzvah*:

Tzaddikim who serve Hashem with feelings created by intellectual contemplation reach the spiritual world of *Briah*, the seat of G-dly intellect (*Bina*).

Malochim (angels) which are lower than souls and serve Hashem with inborn emotion, exist in the world of *Yetzira*, the base of G-dly emotion. *Malochim* are sometimes referred to as "animals" since their conduct is instinctive and not dictated by conscious thought (though some *malochim* were created with mindful emotion and placed in the world of *Briah*).

The *neshama* of a person who serves Hashem with instinctive emotion will merit to ascend to the world of *Yetzira*, which is also called the "lower *Gan Eden*." On special occasions, such as *Shabbos* and *Rosh Chodesh*, they are allowed to enter *Briah*, since (1) they went against their nature and suppressed their desires (*iskafya*), bringing Hashem great pleasure and thus deserving to ascend to great heights. 2) They did it through an intellectual choice to dedicate their emotions towards Hashem. That intellectual element gains them entry to the world of G-dly intellect.

A third and more sublime level is that of total nullification (*bittul bimetzius*) which is beyond reason. This level is only attainable by great *Tzaddikim* who are like a "chariot" for Hashem with selfless devotion. They therefore reach the world of *Atzilus*, which is completely nullified, and receives a ray from Hashem which created beings cannot comprehend (which is why those who served Hashem with comprehension cannot reach it).

All of the above is concerning the *neshama* that performs the *mitzvos*, however the actual Torah and *mitzvos* that a person performs, no matter at which level the person stands, ultimately become totally one with the essence of Hashem Himself. A person who generally served Hashem with intellectual feeling, but sometimes he would reach total nullification (such as during *Shmoneh Esrei*), then his primary position will be in *Briah* (the "higher *Gan Eden*"), but on special days he will ascend to *Atzilus*.

When a person studies Torah without any feeling or intent to serve Hashem, rather because of habit, his Torah ascends only to the external portion of the higher worlds. When he restudies that portion for Hashem's sake, it elevates with it the earlier study as well.

If he studies, however, for selfish reasons (e.g. to gain honor), his Torah is exiled inside that unholy motive. Only through *teshuva* is the Torah released and can ascend above. Our sages taught that a person should always study even for the wrong sake, since we are sure that he will eventually do *teshuva* (even in another lifetime) and elevate that study to its proper place.

"Service without arousal of fear and love remains below."

The Baal Shem Tov once visited a Beis Midrash of those who did not study Chassidus, and he told the scholars that there is a lot of Torah present. They were delighted at the compliment, until he explained that since they did not have love and fear for Hashem, their study remained in that room and did not ascend to its source Above.

CHAPTER 40
Two Wings

———— ∽∼∾ ————

Then a Jew studies Torah with inappropriate intent (such as to be honored), his Torah is covered in *kelipa* and cannot connect with its spiritual source until *teshuva* is done. [If the Torah was studied by habit without any particular intent then it does rise, but remains in the 'external' elements of the higher worlds].

The question begs to be asked: How can the holy Torah, which is essentially one with Hashem, be stuck below and be separate from Hashem?

The answer is that the Torah itself is indeed one with Hashem all the time, however, a person's study uses physical speech which is derived from a very contracted level of G-dliness. When we have the right intent, that physical speech serves as a conduit for holiness and unites with it. But if that intent is lacking, it reverts to its natural state of contracted G-dliness.

That is why the Zohar calls love and fear for Hashem – "wings." Wings are not essential to the life of a bird (and if they are broken, the bird is still *halachically* healthy), and their purpose is only to allow the bird to soar. Likewise, the explicit purpose of G-dly love and fear is, not for their own sake but, to lift up the *mitzvos*.

Now, although love and fear for Hashem are *mitzvos* on their own right, they are nevertheless considered "wings" since they are meant to serve Hashem with love. Feel and taking pleasure in love itself (*ahava b'taanugim*) is a reward and is reserved for the World to Come or for great *Tzaddikim* who have a foretaste in this world.

Those who are not on such a lofty level and still yearn to be near Hashem, can only satisfy that yearning through studying Torah. One who says he is thirsty for Hashem but does not study Torah, is like a person who stands beside a river and cries for water.

"And if not they are called chicks."

It is written in Tikkunei Zohar, "Those who engage in Torah and mitzvos out of fear and love are called 'sons,' but those who engage in Torah and mitzvos without fear and love they are called chicks who cannot fly."

CHAPTERS 41-50:

LEVELS OF LOVE AND FEAR AND THE REFLECTIONS THAT CAUSE THEM

Chapter 41: *The reflection that leads to fear; the need for fear before love.*

Chapter 42: *Advice on how to reach the "lower fear" (yira tata'a).*

Chapter 43: *The reflections that leads to the "higher fear" (yira ila'a), the "great love" (ahava raba), and "love from the world" (ahavas olam).*

Chapter 44: *Two types of natural love - "my soul desires You" and "like a son to a father."*

Chapter 45: *Love from compassion for the neshama.*

Chapters 46-49: Reciprocal Love

Chapter 46: *The meaning of reciprocal love.*

Chapter 47: *Leaving Mitzrayim spiritually each day.*

Chapter 48: *Hashem is infinite.*

Chapter 49: *Hashem limits Himself for our sake and we should limit ourselves for Him.*

Chapter 50: *The advantage of "love like fire."*

CHAPTER 41
Kabbalas Ol

───ᨒ───

*A*fter explaining the significance of action (ch. 35-37) and of feeling (ch. 38-40), the Alter Rebbe begins to explain various levels of love and awe and how to attain each one. But first he explains that between these two emotions, it is awe which begins all G-dly service and continues to be its primary component.

The basis for G-dly service is *kabbalas ol* and awe for Hashem. The first step is for us to accept the yoke of Hashem's kingship: to serve Him because of His command, and not because of a feeling of love to Hashem. Once this foundation is established, we can move forward and develop a feeling of love for Hashem.

Every one of us is capable of uncovering our intuitive awe for Hashem by concentrating on how Hashem, King of the entire universe, sets everything else on the side and focuses on us – to see that we are serving Him fittingly. Every person should reflect upon this for as long as he can, primarily before performing a *mitzvah* or studying Torah.

Another reflection concerns the significance of *mitzvos*, for *Ohr Ein Sof* is enclothed in Torah and *mitzvos* and by performing them we draw down the *Ohr Ein Sof* upon our *neshama*.

Then, there is a reflection regarding the specific *mitzvah* that we are performing. For example, before donning *tefillin* we should consider how the *tefillin* have four sections which correspond to *Chochma*, *Bina*, and the two parts of *Daas* – *Chessed* and *Gevura*. By putting on *tefillin* a Jew's mind becomes united with the *Ohr Ein Sof* so that it becomes dedicated to holy matters. When wrapping ourselves in a *tallis* we should consider that we are drawing upon ourselves Hashem's Kingship.

Even if these reflections don't cause us to be overcome with sensed awe, the thought itself and the conscious acceptance of the yoke of Heaven is considered like actual awe, since essentially every Jew has awe for Hashem buried inside him.

However, if a person doesn't contemplate these topics and accept upon himself the yoke of Heaven, and he studies Torah only out of love for Hashem, he is missing the whole concept of *avoda*, G-dly servitude. The Zohar writes that *mitzvos* without *avoda* lack holiness.

A Jew must be like a "son" and love Hashem, and also like a "servant" with awe for Him, but to be a "son" he must first be a "servant." Love and awe are like wings for a bird: Just as a bird cannot fly with one wing, *mitzvos* need both love and awe to soar Above.

When one does *mitzvos* with proper love of Hashem, his intent is to cling to Hashem through the *mitzvos*.

Moreover, ultimate love for Hashem will result in the desire to bring Hashem pleasure by connecting all of *Klal Yisroel* to Him. This is accomplished by connecting one's *neshama's* source – which is ultimately one with all other *neshamos* – with Hashem Himself.

Although toiling for Hashem's sake alone may seem like a lofty level, it is relevant to every Jew, since deep inside we all have a natural love to Hashem and want to bring Hashem pleasure.

Furthermore, a Jew has a noticeable desire to cling to Hashem through *mitzvos*, as is evident from his willingness to sacrifice his life for Hashem (ch. 18). Every fulfillment of Torah and *mitzvos* is a degree of sacrifice, since one forgoes his own desires and dedicates himself to the will of Hashem.

This intent of self-sacrifice is relevant to Torah study and *mitzvah* performance throughout the day. Since the energy of the world is refreshed every hour (due to the twenty four mutations of Hashem's name), we should stop once an hour and remind himself of this intent.

Yet, we should not be satisfied with our natural love, and we should set aside times to develop intellectual love by contemplating Hashem's greatness.

"Every hour is dominated by one of the twelve mutations of *Havaya*."

When the Alter Rebbe sat in prison, his interrogators wished to test his intelligence. They placed him in a room without windows, and one afternoon, several days later, asked him why he was up since it was in middle of the night. The Alter Rebbe replied that it wasn't night and he told them the exact hour. The officers were taken aback and asked how he knew.

The Rebbe explained that every hour has a different mutation of Hashem's name (twelve by day and another twelve by night), he could tell the time from sensing those spiritual energies.

CHAPTER 42
How to Attain Awe

N ow the Alter Rebbe begins to guide us step-by-step on attaining the various levels of awe and love, beginning with awe.

The key to all emotion is *Daas* – attachment. By intellectually attaching ourselves to a perception of Hashem it becomes real to us, and we can then easily arouse a feeling of awe towards Him.

The main source of *Daas* is Moshe Rabbeinu whose *neshama* is rooted in the supernal *Daas* (*Daas Elyon*) of *Atzilus*. Every Jew has a spark of Moshe within him, and by connecting with that spark, his *Daas*, and consequently his awe, are strengthened.

Furthermore, in each generation there are Jewish leaders who are imbued with Moshe's spirit, and they transfer *Daas* to their students. That *Daas* enables us to contemplate G-dliness and relate to it as we relate to tangible realities. Since the *neshama* is invested in a body, a Jew must toil hard with body and soul – to tame the body by humbling it, and to train the soul to concentrate for long periods of time.

Some refined souls can generate awe instantaneously through minimal contemplation, while coarse souls require great amounts of toiling. However, even the coarsest souls can attain at least some form of awe if they make the effort.

Since every Jew has hidden inborn awe for Hashem, he can reveal it by considering how Hashem watches and hears everything he does and says. The fact that Hashem has no body is only a reason why He can see everything and nothing is hidden from Him.

Just as we know and sense everything that happens to our body, Hashem knows each of His creations. In truth, this parable is not accurate, since the soul is affected by what happens to the body, whereas Hashem is not at all affected by what happens in the world. Still, the parable makes it more comprehendible.

If we consider for a significant period of time on how Hashem watches our every action, we will arouse the awe that is hidden in our heart. A lengthy reflection at the beginning of the day will impact the entire day, so that just reminding ourselves of Hashem's presence will reawaken that awe and stimulate our observance of *mitzvos*.

Another way to become aroused with an awe for Hashem is to contemplate the world and its nature. Just as a person who sees the physical king is filled with awe – though the awe is towards the king's invisible character and not his visible body – so too, when we view the world as the "body" of the G-dly light we will increase our awe of Hashem by looking at the world. And just as watching the king's officers bow to the king inspires awe of the king, so too, observing the planets' subservience to Hashem will arouse within us an awe for Him. Likewise, we should train ourselves to see Hashem as the inner life of the world. In fact, the word *emunah*, faith, is connected to the word *imun*, to train. We will then be capable of accepting the yoke of Heaven.

> ## "Sparks of Moshe Rabbeinu's *neshama* descend into the bodies and souls of the scholars of the generation."
>
> *The spark of Moshe Rabbeinu's neshama becomes enclothed, not only in the souls of the scholars, but also in their bodies. That is why one can satisfy his spiritual yearnings just by gazing at a Tzaddik, since even his body alone contains the spark of Moshe.*

CHAPTER 43
Yira Ila'a, Ahava Raba, and Ahavas Olam

⌇⌇⌇

In the previous chapter, the Alter Rebbe discussed a contemplation of how Hashem is the life of the world. Interacting with the world is only Hashem's external faculty, and considering it elicits only a lower form of awe (*yira tata'a*). Now, the Alter Rebbe will explain how when we can consider Hashem's inner faculty, and how the worlds have no significance at all in comparison to Him, we will be overcome with a deeper sense of awe (*yira ila'a*).

At the first level, the contemplation is regarding the level of G-dliness that creates the world, and this elicits a total dedication to Hashem upon whom he is completely dependent. Yet, because it has a relationship with the world, it does not negate the person's existence entirely. At the second level, we consider the level of

G-dliness which is completely beyond the world. This causes a person to feel completely non-existent.

However, this contemplation will not bring us to *bittul bimetzius* unless we are in complete fulfillment of Torah and *mitzvos*. So the process therefore must be: *yira tata'a* – the lower nullification, which enables us to overcome our *yetzer hara* and fulfill Torah and *mitzvos*, and then *yira ila'a* – the higher nullification.

Now, the Alter Rebbe summarizes the various levels of love:

Ahava raba is a delight in G-dliness, only attainable by one who mastered the higher level of awe of Hashem and is worthy of receiving a gift from Above.

Ahavas olam is a love which comes from contemplating Hashem's greatness, how He is omnipresent, creates everything, and that every being is insignificant in comparison to Him. This will cause a person to view fleeting worldly pleasures as meaningless and to be drawn only to the source of all life – Hashem.

The normal process is for a person to first attain *yirah tata'a*, lower awe, and then *ahavas olam*, love from the world. However, it is possible for a sinner who lacks in fear of Hashem to become aroused with a love for Hashem, which will in turn lead him to do *teshuva* since *ahavas olam* contains an element of awe from Hashem's greatness.

To Want the Real Thing

There is a saying that the difference between children and adults is the cost of their toys. A child wants a toy car, but when he grows older he wants the real thing; a toy car is now petty.

Similarly, if we educate our Animalistic Soul that G-dliness is the "real thing" and the world is only a "toy" in comparison, we will naturally desire G-dliness over worldly pleasures.

CHAPTER 44
Two Types of Inborn Love

———— ~∽~ ————

This chapter will discuss two types of inborn natural love which every Jew has, both of which include both levels of love mentioned in the previous chapter – *ahavas olam* and *ahava raba*.

The first is called "My soul desires You" (*nafshi ivisicha*) based on the Zohar's interpretation of that *passuk* that Dovid HaMelech speaks both of his desire for Hashem and his desire for his own soul. With this he wished to say that just as a person desires his own "soul" (his life), and this desire permeates every aspect of one's life, so too, every Jew has an inborn desire to be connected to Hashem which he will feel every moment of his life.

In the second level, a person relates to Hashem like a son who is prepared to do anything for his parents, and he loves them even more than he loves his own self. Such a selfless love for Hashem is truly exceptional, and the

Zohar attributes it to Moshe Rabbeinu, yet, every Jew has a fragment of that love within him.

By habituating oneself to relate to Hashem as his own father, it will become second nature. Although the lofty emotion is not entirely genuine and is seemingly imaginary, it should not concern us, since, in the depths of our heart this sentiment truly exist.

These two loves seem to stem from our natural love. However, when they are aroused by the means of these contemplations (that Hashem is our Life and our Father), it has the advantage of intellectual love. If that contemplation arouses our heart, it causes the *mitzvos* to ascend, not only to the world of emotion (*Yetzira*), but even to the world of intellect (*Briah*).

Furthermore, these two forms of love have the advantage of *ahava raba* which is even greater than intellectual love and raises *mitzvos* to the world of *Atzilus*.

Nevertheless, one should still consider Hashem's greatness and develop *ahavas olam* for two reasons: (1) Intellectual love leads to a fiery love of yearning for Hashem, while natural love only breeds a love "like water" – a feeling of closeness to Hashem (explained in ch. 50). (2) The Zohar states that the purpose of man's creation is to intellectually understand the Creator.

"By visualizing this love in his mind."

The Frierdiker Rebbe said: "Through visualizing, a person can reach lofty levels and feelings, which he could never reach with intellect. While deep thought often causes a disconnect from reality, visualizing brings a person closer to reality, and the matter becomes engraved, not only in his spiritual faculties, but also in his physical ones."

CHAPTER 45
Compassion Which Arouses Love

In the end of the previous chapter it was noted that there is a love "like water" and a love "like fire." These two correspond to *chessed* (Avraham's trait) and *gevura* (Yitzchak's trait). Now the Alter Rebbe explains a third type of love which results from the third *mida* of *rachmanus*, compassion (Yaakov's trait).

Compassion is aroused by considering how our *neshama* descended from its state of closeness to Hashem in the higher spiritual worlds into a body in this physical world which conceals Hashem's presence. If a person is involved in unholy matters his *neshama* is subject to even further descent, and this rouses even more compassion. This compassion for his *neshama's* sorry state will inspire us to yearn for Hashem.

This explains why Yaakov kissed Rochel and cried. Rochel represents *knesses yisroel*, the source of *neshamos*, and Yaakov represents the supernal compassion. By crying, Yaakov aroused compassion for all future *neshamos*, thereby taking them out of their spiritual bondage. He then united them with Hashem, through kissing, which indicates a tight connection. This connection is achieved today through studying Torah, especially *halacha*. Another form of attachment is embracing, which is caused primarily through acts of kindness and *tzedaka*.

"Yaakov who redeemed Avraham."

The Gemara explains that Yaakov redeemed Avraham by bearing him many descendants. The Midrash explains that Yaakov's merit spared Avraham from the fire at Ur Kasdim.

Here the Alter Rebbe explains that Yaakov's trait of compassion redeems Avraham's trait of love. When our love for Hashem is hidden, we can uncover it through compassion.

CHAPTER 46
The Meaning of Reciprocal Love

———— ✺ ————

There is yet another way to arouse the natural love buried within the heart of every Jew. With just a small amount of thought it can easily be uncovered and fanned into a burning love.

Human nature is such that when someone shows us love, we respond with love to them. Even more so when the one showing us love is greater than us. For example, if a great king, along with all of his ministers visits a lowly tramp, takes him out of the filthy gutter, brings him to the palace, and invites him into his private chamber – surely this man will feel an incredible love for the king. Even if his heart is hard like stone, it would melt from such loving care.

In our case, the king is Hashem and we are that lowly person. Hashem descended from His lofty level into

Mitzrayim – a decadent land within this lowly world – in order to give us the Torah. Reflecting upon Hashem's great love for us will stir within us a love for Hashem.

Studying Torah and fulfilling *mitzvos* connects both of our souls with Hashem's Infinite Light. That is why the *bracha* over a *mitzvah* begins, "*asher kidshanu*," Who has made us holy, for through *mitzvos* we become holy and united with Hashem. *Kidshanu* has the implication of *kiddushin*, the betrothal of a husband and wife. *Kidshanu* also means "separated," since when we study Torah or do a *mitzvah* we unite with Hashem as He is separate and higher than the world.

For this reason, we are commanded to stand up before even an ordinary person who performs a *mitzvah*, since while he does the *mitzvah*, Hashem rests in him. Since we are mortal we do not sense it, however, that doesn't change the reality. Likewise, one who doesn't sense the holiness of *Shabbos* may not perform work the same as a righteous person, since the holy spirit of *Shabbos* rests upon every Jew whether he feels it or not.

Connected through a *Mitzvah*

The passuk says: "I am like an animal before You. [Yet] I am continually with You." The inner meaning of this is: Even a simple person who doesn't have a true understanding and feeling for G-dliness, and is likened to an "animal," he is still "with You" – connected to Hashem in the highest form through preforming a mitzvah.

CHAPTER 47
Leaving Mitzrayim Each Day

Although the physical exodus from *Mitzrayim* occurred thousands of years ago, we are told to feel as having been redeemed from *Mitzrayim* every day, since indeed we are freed spiritually on a daily basis. Whenever we study Torah, do a *mitzvah* or accept upon ourselves the yoke of Heaven in *Shema*, we free our *neshama* of the body's captivity. The exodus from *Mitzrayim* is appended to *Shema* since reciting *Shema* is about going free from our own spiritual bondage.

Hashem invested Himself inside the Torah and gave it to us as a gift, thereby giving us Himself. Every one of us can unite with Hashem, and it is only our own will that can hold us back.

"As it says in Zohar on the *passuk*, '*veyikchu li terumah*,' 'and they should take for Me a portion.'"

The word "li" in the passuk is usually translated as "for Me." The Zohar explains it as "Me," meaning that the Jews will take Hashem, so to speak, and "terumah" refers to the Torah which we take. According to this understanding, the passuk should have read, "li uterumah," which would mean that we take Hashem and the Torah. Why isn't there an "and" separating the two?

The implication is that only one thing is being taken. Since Hashem and the Torah are one, when we take the Torah, we take Hashem.

CHAPTER 48
Hashem's Greatness

In the previous chapters, the Alter Rebbe explained how like a king who lowers himself to lift up a lowly person, Hashem's descended below to remove us from *Mitzrayim*. He also explained how redemption from *Mitzrayim* was not a one-time incident, but a daily occurrence. Here the Alter Rebbe will explain the great descent which Hashem makes today to free us from our spiritual bondage.

Ohr Ein Sof, Hashem's infinite light, is literally infinite and limitless. In order to create defined worlds, the infinite light had to be contracted (*tzimtzum*) so that only a small ray remains. The difference between the light 'before' the *tzimtzum* and 'afterwards' is like the difference between a finite number and infinity; they have no comparison to each other whatsoever.

The light of Hashem the way it is without the impact of the *tzimtzum* is called "*sovev kol almin*," surrounding the worlds. Although it penetrates every world and there is no space void of it, it is too lofty to be revealed, and its effect on the world is hidden.

In order for there to be different classes within creation – inanimate, plants, animals and humans – another more limited light is needed, which can become enclothed and suit itself to each type of being.

CHAPTER 49
Reciprocal Love

I n this chapter, the Alter Rebbe concludes his discussion about the reciprocal love which results from our recognizing Hashem's love for us.

The previous chapter explained how *Ohr Ein Sof*, Hashem's infinite light, is too intense for the world to handle, and in order to create the world the light has to be contracted (*tzimtzum*). Three primary *tzimtzumim* are necessary to create the three worlds of *Briah*, *Yetzira* and *Asiya*. The final product is a material world with human beings who experience material lusts. The purpose of this contraction is that we should overcome our desires and transform the darkness into light.

When we contemplate how Hashem, out of His great love for us, contracts Himself into our lowly predicament to enable us to connect to Him, we are inspired to limit ourselves for Hashem's sake. We become willing to set everything aside in order to cleave to Hashem.

With this, we can understand the connection between the *brachos* before *Shema* and *Shema* itself. The purpose of *Shema* is to love Hashem and give everything up for Him. The first *bracha* speaks of the *malochim's* nullification to Hashem, and the second speaks of Hashem's exceptional love for us. The way that a person prepares to give everything up for Hashem is by first contemplating how great Hashem is and then contemplating how Hashem in all of His greatness puts everything aside (as it were) out of His love for us.

After reciting the first *psukim* of *Shema* which discuss our willingness to give up everything for Hashem, we continue with *psukim* that discuss actual Torah learning and *mitzvah* observance, since true closeness to Hashem, is achieved specifically through performing the physical *mitzvos*.

Eitz Hachayim

In this perek the Alter Rebbe refers to those with a knowledge of Kabbalah as those who have "tasted from the Eitz Hachayim (the tree of life)." Kabbalah is called "tree of life" because it does not discuss mundane matters like the revealed portion of Torah, but rather it discusses Hashem, the true "life."

CHAPTER 50
Love like Fire

~~~

In the previous chapters, the Alter Rebbe spoke of various levels in "love like water," a composed love to Hashem which inspires a person to increase in observing *mitzvos*. Now, he discusses a love, which like fire, burns with a desire to escape and come closer to Hashem.

In this chapter, the Alter Rebbe describes one such love which results from contemplating Hashem's Essence which is so far beyond us. When we consider how Hashem is higher than all of the worlds and how they are all like nothing before Him, we will become fired up with a burning thirst to expire and unite with Hashem.

Unlike "love like water," this love by itself will not motivate us to fulfill *mitzvos* since, on the contrary, it inspires us to want to escape from this finite world. That is why this yearning, *ratzui*, must be followed by a return, *shov*, in which we force ourselves to carry out what Hashem wants us to accomplish in this world.

Silver and Gold

The advantage of "love like fire" over "love like water" is compared to the advantage of gold over silver. Gold is not just better than silver, but is an entirely different realm. So too "love like fire" is on an entirely different level than "love like water."

CHAPTERS 51-53:

THE ABODE OF THE SHECHINA

Chapter 51: *The body and soul as an analogy for Hashem and the world.*

Chapter 52: *The Shechina rests in Torah.*

Chapter 53: *Torah and mitzvos draw the Shechina into the world.*

CHAPTER 51
Revealing the Neshama

———— ~~~~ ————

*A*fter guiding us in great detail on how to attain
awe and love for Hashem (ch. 41-50), the Alter
Rebbe concludes the book with an explanation on the
Zohar's statement (brought in ch. 35) that the light of
the *Shechina* lights as a result of "oil" – which is a parable
for *mitzvos*. This will lead to the conclusion that action
is the main thing. Here the Alter Rebbe will explain the
connection between "oil," which is known to correspond
to *Chochma*, and *mitzvos*.

We know that the *Shechina* rested in the *Kodesh
Hakodoshim* of the *Beis Hamikdash*. How does this fit
with the fact that Hashem fills the entire world?

The Alter Rebbe answers this question with a parable
of the soul and the body – on the one hand, the soul is
said to rest in the mind, and on the other hand, the soul
itself exists in every part of the body. Both are true: the
soul itself is present in the entire body, but its expression
and function varies from limb to limb – the eyes see, the

ears hear, and so on. The transitional stage between the abstract soul and its specific functions is the soul as it is expressed in the mind.

The same is true of the expression of *Ohr Ein Sof* in the world. Hashem's essence exists everywhere equally, like the soul's essence. The difference between the higher and lower worlds is in how much is revealed to them: the higher worlds receive a greater revelation than the lower ones. Each creation receives a life-force which is suited for it. The outcome is a physical world where Hashem isn't visible despite the fact that He recreates it every moment.

> ## "Each limb receives energy from the soul according to its character."
>
> *The Rebbe explains that one could have thought that the neshama provides the same energy to every limb, and the different functions of the various organs is due to the specific qualities of those organs. The Alter Rebbe therefore emphasizes that the life-force itself varies according to the needs of the organs.*

CHAPTER 52
Hashem's Revelation in Torah

———— ᴎᵔᴎ ————

The Alter Rebbe continues to explain the parable: The mind, as explained, contains the soul as it is applied and expressed, but before it is limited to a specific function. Similarly, the primary revelation of *Elokus* is in Hashem's "mind," which is the *sefira* of *Chochma* and other elements of the G-dly "intellect" (*Kesser, Bina, Daas*). From the "mind" it descends to the "emotions" until the final *sefira* of *Malchus*, which is the bridge to the world below it.

Malchus of *Atzilus* is called *Shechina*, "dwelling," since it is the first G-dly revelation which can dwell in the lower worlds (below *Atzilus*). This revelation could not be openly revealed since then the worlds would lose their autonomy and existence. Instead, the *Shechina* was hidden in Hashem's Will and Thought – the Torah –

which comes from *Chochma* of *Atzilus* and descended into physical matters.

Every world has its "intellect" which houses the *Shechina* and distributes it to that world. In the spiritual worlds it is the first *Sefiros*, and in our physical world, when the Beis Hamikdash stood, it was the Kodesh Hakodoshim.

"And this source is called '*Alma D'Isgalaya*,' the revealed world."

In seforim of Kabbalah, the source for the world is called, "Alma D'Isgalaya," the revealed world, since it is the source for the initial revelation of Ohr Ein Sof.

In Zohar it is known as, "Matrunisa," queen, since this level receives from the King, Hashem, to give life to the world. It is also known as "Eima Tata'a," the lower mother, because it is the source of all neshamos, like a mother gives birth to children.

In Gemara it is referred to as "Shechina," since it rests in the world.

In Kabbalah this level is called, "Malchus of Atzilus."

"The *halachos* themselves are from Hashem's attributes of Kindness, Judgment, and Mercy."

What's the connection between halachic rulings and the supernal attributes?

A halachic ruling, the instruction of what is permissible and prohibited, is an expression of love or fear. halacha tells us what Hashem likes and dislikes, and with our love for Him we follow His instructions.

CHAPTER 53
The Main Thing is Action

———～⌒～———

During the time of the first Beis Hamikdash, the *Shechina* was openly revealed in the Kodesh Hakodoshim. This was expressed in the *luchos* that had G-dly writing on a physical object. The second Beis Hamikdash didn't have the *aron* and the *luchos* and the revelation was therefore of a lower nature. Since the destruction of the Beis Hamikdash the *Shechina* has transferred to the Torah, as *Chazal* say that every individual who studies Torah "the *Shechina* is with him."

More specifically, the *Shechina* is drawn through practicing the *mitzvos*, since they are the ultimate goal of the Torah. Even the study of Torah and the recital of *brachos* and *davening* require the physical movement of the lips. The *Shechina* is particularly drawn down through the study of *Torah Sheba'al Peh* where the laws of Torah are specified in detail.

This is the meaning of the Zohar that oil is needed for the *Shechina* to light. Oil refers to *Chochma* and

Torah, and is also expressed in *mitzvos*. The wick, which is the Animalistic Soul, becomes transformed to fire and it illuminates when it is soaked with the "oil."

Even the *Beinoni* who hasn't transformed his Animalistic Soul itself, can nonetheless illuminate its thought, speech and action through *mitzvos*. Thereby, he illuminates the world at large.

"The *luchos* were the handiwork of Hashem."

Although the luchos were made of physical matter, they were not essentially physical. They were formed directly by Hashem, and did not develop through a process like all other creations. For this reason, the lettering in the luchos superseded the laws of nature: the center of the samech and of the final mem hung in mid-air. Also, the letters of the luchos were engraved through and through, and one could read the writing on the opposite side in the correct order.

"Every word of Tanya was written with *mesiras nefesh*."

The Frierdiker Rebbe said:

There is "joy set in one side of my heart" from the fact that Tanya is studied, but yet there is "crying set in the other side of my heart" from its being viewed as a book of moral guidance or philosophy.

Tanya is neither; it is a "Torah Shebiksav," and every word in Tanya was written with sweat of mesiras nefesh. You study Tanya, and you must therefore consider how you appear before you study it and how you appear afterwards, how it has influenced you, and how it affected your "closing your eyes and ears [from seeing or hearing evil]."

(Sefer HaSichos, Winter 5700, p. 360)

General Summary

Chapters 18-25:
Uncovering the Hidden Love

Chapters 26-34:
Finding Joy and Banishing Sadness

Chapters 35-40:
Action vs. Meaning

לזכות

חנה, לוי יצחק, משה חיים, אודל וחיה מושקא

נדפס ע"י הוריהם

הרה"ח ר' יעקב זאב ומעיין אלבליה
שיחיו

שיזכו לראות נחת חסידי אמיתי
והצלחה רבה ומופלגה
בכל מעשי ידיהם

Made in the USA
Middletown, DE
06 March 2022

62242243R00096